YOURGIFTS

DISCOVER GOD'S UNIQUE DESIGN FOR YOU

Includes the Easy-to-Use, Self-Guided
SPIRITUAL GIFTS SURVEY
FOR INDIVIDUALS AND GROUPS

DEVELOPED BY
DR. LARRY GILBERT

ChurchGrowth.org
Timeless Tools for Christian Growth

Your Gifts
Copyright © 2015 ChurchGrowth.org

Revised and edited by Kyle Duncan and Cindy Spear
Designed by Peter Gloege

Unless otherwise noted, all Scripture quotations are taken from the HOLY BIBLE: NEW INTERNATIONAL VERSION®. © 1973, 1978, 1984 by International Bible Society. Used by permission of Zondervan Publishing House. All rights reserved.

Scripture quotations marked KJV are taken from the Holy Bible, *King James Version,* Cambridge, 1769.

Scripture quotations marked NASB are taken from the New American Standard Bible®, Copyright © 1960, 1962, 1963, 1968, 1971, 1972, 1973, 1975, 1977, 1995 by The Lockman Foundation. (www.Lockman.org)

Published by ChurchGrowth.org
Forest, Virginia, USA

Team Ministry is a registered trademark of ChurchGrowth.org.
Any use of this name is prohibited without the express written consent of ChurchGrowth.org.

Library of Congress Cataloging-in-Publication Data

Gilbert, Larry
Your Gifts : Discover God's unique design for you/ Larry Gilbert

p. cm.

ISBN 978-1-57052-289-5
     978-1-57052-334-2 (eBook)

Printed in the United States of America
22 21 20 19 18 17 16 15   1 2 3 4 5 6 7 8 9 10 11 12

FOREWORD

Spiritual gifts are key ingredients to building an effective, growing church. The key phrase is "using people where they are usable." If all Christians were involved according to their spiritual gifts, they would be used in ministering where they are most usable. I find that growing churches cannot be dis-associated from growing Christians. Therefore, when Christians find their gifts, know the significance of their gifts and properly exercise their gifts, they will grow. As the people grow (internal growth) then the church will grow (external growth).

I believe the TEAM Ministry resources by Larry Gilbert are the best materials written on spiritual gifts. The concepts of TEAM Ministry, and the truths found here in *Your Gifts,* will build a strong foundation in a local church, inspire leadership, motivate laypeople, and turn declining churches around.

TEAM Ministry is the result of more than thirty years of study, research and observation of church ministries by Larry Gilbert. I have worked with him and we have had long discussions in the area of spiritual gifts. We have worked together on numerous church growth projects—programs that were never just gimmicks or campaigns, but were built on church growth principles and the use of spiritual gifts.

Larry Gilbert understands the foundation of spiritual gifts for church growth, personal ministry, and daily living. Therefore, this book will make a significant contribution for individuals, pastors, and leaders to help them strengthen their daily walk and build up the church to the glory of God.

Dr. Elmer Towns,
Vice President and Co-Founder, Liberty University

HOW TO USE THIS BOOK

*"Therefore go and make disciples of all nations, baptizing them
in the name of the Father and of the Son and of the Holy Spirit,
and teaching them to obey everything I have commanded you.
And surely I am with you always, to the very end of the age."*
—MATTHEW 28:19-20

The Great Commission is the greatest command, given by the greatest Commander, to the greatest army, for the greatest task ever. Although many churches have argued it, debated it, denied it, and ignored it, most have accepted it as their marching orders. Outreach, evangelism, and reaching people for Christ have become the very heartbeat of most churches. We have recognized this task and boldly set out to accomplish this seemingly unreachable goal of taking the Gospel to the world. In fact, the whole philosophy of ministry in most evangelical churches evolves from—and revolves around—the Great Commission, "the Great Task."

The God who assigned us this great task also provided us the means to fulfill the task—a TEAM of people (the local church), men and women whom God has equipped to fulfill that task, men and women with God-given spiritual gifts. TEAM Ministry includes everyone in that task, without forcing anyone to be someone they are not.

The "TEAM" in TEAM Ministry is not a committee in the church, a small group taken from the whole, or a special taskforce; but rather the TEAM is *all* the members of the local church; the local church itself.

TEAM Ministry revolves around people and their God-given gifts, not just the task. The basis of TEAM Ministry is expressed in four themes:

1. God gave the Great Commission to the church and has equipped the body to fulfill it collectively through a gifted, informed, understanding, and cooperating TEAM.

2. When individual believers discover their spiritual gifts, they will become more effective, more efficient, and fulfilled as they serve on God's local church TEAM.

3. TEAM Ministry is fundamental to the believer, to the ministry, to the church, and to both qualitative and quantitative church growth.

4. Recognizing, understanding, and implementing TEAM Ministry as spiritual-gift-based ministry is a key ingredient to equipping, preparing, and motivating laypeople to do the work of the ministry.

This book was written to properly identify that God-gifted workforce and teach it to grow, become involved in ministry, and mature into the image of Christ, bringing it together to fulfill the God-given task of reaching a lost world. Our goal here is not only to help every user determine their spiritual gift(s) but to help leaders structure their churches in a manner that allows every member to serve in an area of ministry that complements their gifts. In doing so, leaders will be able to create maximum effectiveness and efficiency *and* maximum fulfillment with minimum frustration for each member while equipping them to serve God.

TEAM Ministry positions church leaders to equip the laity to fulfill the Great Commission (see Ephesians 4:11-12, 2 Timothy 2:2, Matthew 28:19-20).

GETTING THE MOST FROM YOUR GIFTS

We must do more than learn the definitions, characteristics and principles of spiritual gifts; we must put them into practice in daily living and service for God. Therefore, at the close of every chapter you will find a section titled **Next Steps.** In this wrap-up section, a conclusion is drawn from the material presented in the chapter. The purpose of this section is to help you understand how to personally and practically apply that chapter in your life and church. As you work through this book, be sure to ask God to guide you in identifying, understanding, and using your spiritual gifts for His purpose and glory.

The book is split into two parts:

Part 1 – Chapters 1-8 cover the practical description and understanding of TEAM-oriented spiritual gifts.

Part 2 – In Chapters 9-17, each of the nine spiritual gifts is covered in depth. You will learn how to activate your particular gift(s) in your own life, and to encourage others to unlock their spiritual gifts as well.

HOW TO LEAD A GROUP USING THIS BOOK

This book is meant to be used and re-used—as a tool for the reader, the leader or church worker, and as a tool that allows you to equip those in your church or sphere of influence to understand and activate their spiritual gifts. In that sense, this book is meant to be a companion to the *Your Gifts* Spiritual Gifts Survey included in this book (starting on page 173).

As you will see, each chapter also includes two study options:

For Personal Reflection questions to help you internalize the principles shared. Discuss during your small group, or encourage students to study at home on their own (depending upon time constraints).

For Group Discussion questions so you can teach the material in a Sunday school, small group, or home group setting to arm students with the life-changing principles of spiritual gifts activation. In both study sections, you will see space for writing. Please write in this book—and encourage those in your group or class to write in their books as well.

Though you can administer the *Your Gifts* Spiritual Gifts Survey separately to those in your church or under your leadership, it is highly recommended that each participant purchase and read

9

this book, written precisely for laypeople. If some members do not have access to their own copy of this book, you can purchase copies of the *Your Gifts* Spiritual Gifts Survey wherever Christian books and resources are sold.

Ideally, within the small group, each member (leaders and each participant) will have taken the *Your Gifts* Spiritual Gifts Survey before beginning the class, and prior to reading *Your Gifts* (for individuals and laypeople) or *Team Ministry* (for leaders). In this way, participants will begin the small group already aware of their spiritual gifts, and will be able to maximize the content of *Your Gifts* for deeper understanding and effectiveness

Feel free to customize this material as you see fit. For example, each of the eight chapters in Part I include a study section at the end (including a list of the answers, on page 183). Depending upon how long you wish to study the spiritual gifts in a group setting, you could read and discuss one chapter per week for an eight-week study, or have your students read two chapters per week and cover the material over four weeks. The material could also be taught in a one-day seminar or retreat setting. The choice is yours, though we encourage you to cover just one chapter per week, if possible.

If you have any questions about the various TEAM Ministry spiritual gifts books and resources, please visit us at www.ChurchGrowth.org for more information.

PART 1

UNDERSTANDING
THE TEAM GIFTS

MUCH MATERIAL IS AVAILABLE
TO HELP PEOPLE RECOGNIZE,
DISCOVER, AND DEFINE THEIR
PARTICULAR SPIRITUAL GIFTS.
MOST CHRISTIANS, HOWEVER, DO NOT
UNDERSTAND THE RELATIONSHIPS
OF SPIRITUAL GIFTS—HOW A
SPIRITUAL GIFT RELATES TO
THEIR LIVES, OTHER PEOPLE'S LIVES,
THE LOCAL CHURCH OR TO THE
BODY OF CHRIST AS A WHOLE.

1

EIGHT REASONS WHY EVERY CHRISTIAN SHOULD KNOW THEIR SPIRITUAL GIFT

Once at a Sunday school convention I taught two workshops, *"Teaching Spiritual Gifts in the Sunday School"* and *"How to Discover Your Spiritual Gift."* The "teaching" workshop attracted 30 people while the "discovery" workshop attracted about 150 people, both to a room that seated 35. People are curious and long to discover more about themselves. Approximately 100 people stood willingly during the hour-long presentation hoping to discover their spiritual gifts.

Much material is available to help people recognize, discover, and define their particular spiritual gifts. Most Christians, however, do not understand the *relationships* of spiritual gifts–how a spiritual gift relates to their lives, other people's lives, the local church or to the body of Christ as a whole. Therefore, identifying *and* understanding God-given spiritual gift(s) should be a high priority in every Christian's life. Likewise, pastors who understand spiritual gifts in light of their relationship to other areas of ministry will better understand their own roles.

Here are eight reasons why identifying *and* understanding your God-given spiritual gift(s), and the gifts of those around you, should be a high priority.

1. Knowing your spiritual gift helps you understand God's will for your life. Spiritual gifts are tools given by God for doing the work of the ministry. Different people are given different gifts to handle different tasks. For example, if God gives you a hammer, He wants you to drive nails, not cut boards. If He wanted you to cut boards, He would have given you a saw rather than a hammer.

Different people are given different gifts to handle different tasks.

Understanding your gift in light of this principle will enable you to make decisions about where to serve God, how to serve Him, and in many cases, help you choose your occupation. But in all cases it will help you set priorities for your life. *What God has called you to do He has gifted you to do, and what He has gifted you to do He has called you to do.*

2. Knowing your spiritual gift helps you know what God has not called you to do. After selling my business of fourteen years, selling my home, moving my wife and three children 300 miles away to prepare for the ministry, probably the greatest discovery I ever made was that God had *not* called me to become a pastor.

The more I understand what God *has not* called me to do, the more I understand what He *has* called me to do. No doubt, recognizing what you are not supposed to do can be as important as recognizing what you are to do.

If you realize God has not given you the gift of "mercy," you can easily turn down a position that would require that gift, without worrying that you might miss God's calling. The same is true with all the gifts.

3. Knowing your spiritual gift relieves you from serving out of "duty." If the truth were known, many active church workers have no business doing what they are doing. They are only doing it because the pastor asked them to, a committee elected them, or they feel obligated to do something; but they are not serving where they were gifted.

Christians have many reasons for serving in areas that keep them busy but not fulfilled. It boils down to this: many serve out of *duty* instead of *God's calling.* By discovering and utilizing your God-given gifts, it will reduce your chances of serving out of duty, and allow you to serve through the joy of your calling.

4. Knowing your spiritual gift helps you understand how the Holy Spirit works through you. God has chosen people through which to do His work here on earth. Dr. Elmer Towns teaches a principle he calls "the division of labor," based on 1 Corinthians 3:9, which states, "For we are laborers together with God." His principle simply states that "God will not do what He has commanded you to do, and you cannot do what God has reserved as His authority." Certain areas of ministering to people are reserved as His authority or duty. Certain areas of ministering to people are reserved by God to be done by people, and God will not step into these prescribed boundaries to do your job for you.

For instance, in Luke 6:38, Luke pens, "Give (meaning, you give to God's work), and it shall be given unto you; good measure, pressed down, and shaken together, and running over, shall men give into your bosom" (KJV). God's method for giving His people material rewards here on earth is *through people*. There won't be any pennies from heaven; just God's faithful servants rewarding as He directs.

Spiritual gifts are God's provision for the Holy Spirit to minister to people, through people. Without spiritual gifts people can minister one to another only in the flesh. You and I are the only vessels the Holy Spirit uses to accomplish His work here on earth. We must yield ourselves to the Spirit and learn as much as we can about how the Holy Spirit works through us. Years ago I received a little desk plaque from Millhuff Ministries, which sums it up best, "God can if I will."

5. Knowing your spiritual gift fills a deep inner need or void in your life.

Have you ever visited a hospital? You may have met the mean old nurse who bites your head off every time you sit on a patient's bed. But overall, a hospital is a place where you find a staff of people who are getting more fulfillment out of life than the average person. Why? Because they are in the "people-serving business." They are willing to wrap their lives in the lives of other people. They are meeting an inner need that God has put into the souls of all people, Christians and non-Christians alike. Your spiritual gift will complement this inner need God has placed in you.

Certain areas of ministering to people are reserved by God to be done by people, and God will not step into these prescribed boundaries to do your job for you.

Stop and think for a minute of the most miserable, unhappy person you know. Without a doubt that person is very self-centered and only does for others when it benefits him or her in return.

15

6. Knowing your spiritual gift builds unity among Christians. When you understand the characteristics of spiritual gifts, you see how gifts influence your desires, motivation, and behavior. You will begin to realize why other people do not always see things, or react to a situation, the same as you would. It's all part of God's plan. The different gifts complement each other.

A young lady approached me at a seminar I was teaching and said, "Now that I understand my husband's spiritual gifts, I understand why he is so willing to jump in and help family and neighbors with a multitude of projects around their homes." Her husband had the gift of Serving and received true fulfillment by working with his hands and helping others.

Understanding spiritual gifts will also prevent you from imposing your gift or lifestyle on others and will help you recognize God's individual calling for your life. Unfortunately, too many Christians are living God's will for someone else's life rather than their own.

7. Knowing your spiritual gift equips you to fulfill God's purpose for your life. Rick Warren's book *The Purpose Driven Life* became the number one best-selling hardback book of all time (other than the Bible). Since its publication in 2002, combined hard cover and trade paper sales have topped 32 million copies. Why? Because people find a real void in their lives and feel they lack purpose. Understanding your spiritual gifts gives you a clearer understanding of God's purpose for your life. God has created each one of us uniquely and has given us different gifts, talents, personalities, temperaments, and passions to outfit us to accomplish His unique purpose for each of us. True significance in life comes when we discover and apply that purpose and calling.

Unfortunately, too many Christians are living God's will for someone else's life rather than their own.

Introducing spiritual gifts in Ephesians 4:1, Paul exhorts us to "walk worthy of the vocation wherewith ye are called" (KJV). Today when we use the term "vocation" we are referring to our job or career. But in Bible times and in the Scriptures it goes far beyond career. It actually takes in all aspects of our life, career, family, ministry, hobbies, etc. It's our *calling* in life. In fact, later translations of Scripture define the word "vocation" as "calling." Your calling in life is the

16

purpose for which God made you. It has been said, "Career is what you're paid for, but calling is what you're made for."

8. Knowing your spiritual gift adds to your self-acceptance. Recently, a man who had just discovered his spiritual gift and its effect on his life expressed to me, "I love to teach, and I teach every chance I get—I've never done anything in the church but teach. I really don't want to do anything but teach, nor do I intend to do anything but teach. If I go for any period of time without teaching, I become irritable and hard to get along with. I've taught for years, but you know something, for the first time in my life *I don't feel guilty* because I'm not pastoring a church."

Later translations of Scripture define the word "vocation" as "calling." Your calling in life is the purpose for which God made you.

Undue guilt is the greatest tool Satan uses to keep Christians from living up to their potential. Many believers consider themselves unspiritual because they cannot live up to someone else's expectations. Trying to live up to others' expectations of you always equals failure if your expectations are not in line with what *God* expects of you.

Think of the greatest Christian you know. Now consider this: God has called you to do what this person *cannot* do. Your God has given you a special endowment that suits you perfectly for your special position on the TEAM. The Christian who knows he has the gift of Serving will not belittle himself because he is not a pastor. He can accept himself knowing his Lord has given him a special endowment that suits him perfectly for this special position on the TEAM. The Christian who knows that her gift is Administration, and is functioning effectively in her capacity, will not think herself unworthy or unnecessary because she is not a Teacher.

PURSUING GOD'S STEWARDSHIP

In reality, spiritual gifts involve *God's stewardship*. He assigns us certain tasks (see 1 Corinthians 12:18), and then equips us to do them in a manner that brings glory to Him and fulfillment to us (see 1 Peter 4:10-11).

When we think of stewardship we automatically think of finances and material resources. But the parallel between gifts and finances is remarkably

17

the same. Many Christians think that God has commanded us to tithe and give to the church because the church wouldn't be able to function, support it's ministries, and pay its bills otherwise. But the God who owns the cattle on a thousand hills could surely finance His ministry in other ways if He wished. The truth is, when we do not give we are incomplete as a person.

(Only a person who has been tithing for some time can truly understand this principle.)

God could send a legion of angels to do his work here on earth. But, he doesn't. He elected to use you and me.

The same is true with spiritual gifts. God could send a legion of angels to do his work here on earth. But, he doesn't. He elected to use you and me because if we are not using our gifts to serve others we are incomplete and will never receive the blessing and fulfillment He has in store for us.

A young man received an envelope from his grandfather upon graduation from high school. He decided not to open it until he had finished college. After all, he knew it contained bonds promised him for years. So he decided to discipline himself by keeping them to help start his career rather than using them for college. So for four long years he attended school during the day and worked evenings and nights. Finally the day he had restrained himself for had come. With degree in hand, ready to start his new career, he opened the gift his grandfather had left for him years before. Just as he had anticipated, it contained several thousand dollars worth of negotiable bonds; but to his dismay, it also contained a fully paid scholarship to one of the finest colleges in the land.

God has also given you a gift, but it is up to you whether or not you open it. It is your birthday present, given to you by God at the time of your spiritual birth. Once you open it and examine it, you too may be surprised. Don't miss out on the blessings God has for you. Your challenge is two-fold. First, you are to do as commanded in 2 Timothy 1:6: "Therefore I remind you to stir up the gift of God which is in you" (KJV). And second, to do as admonished in 1 Peter 4:10: "As each one has received a gift, minister it to one another, as good stewards of the manifold grace of God" (KJV).

NEXT STEPS

Once you have identified your dominant spiritual gift(s), begin to discover and understand how that gift relates to your life, other people's lives, the local church, and the body of Christ as a whole. Some ways to do this include exercising your gift, paying attention to how your gift might affect your vocation, paying attention to how other people's gifts are evident in their lives, studying about gifts, looking for how the different gifts relate or fit into everyday life and ministry, and becoming aware of ministry opportunities and considering how your gift might play a role.

Review the eight reasons why every Christian should know their spiritual gift and apply them to yourself. By better understanding and exercising your gift(s), you will begin to fulfill God's purpose for you. Be a good steward of the gifts and responsibilities God has entrusted to you. Remember to press forward to do what God has gifted and called you to do. Don't let someone else's expectations of you stand in the way of God's best for you.

19

FOR PERSONAL REFLECTION

1. What do most Christians *not* understand about spiritual gifts?

2. Spiritual gifts are tools to be used for what?

3. What are some reasons Christians should know their spiritual gifts?

4. What do you believe God has gifted you to do? How is this evident in your life?

5. What is something specific you know that God has not called you to do? What is something that He has called you to do? What led you to these conclusions?

6. How do you believe understanding your God-given spiritual gift(s) will help you?

FOR GROUP DISCUSSION

Knowing your spiritual gift . . .

1. . . . helps you understand the _____.

   "What God has called you to do, He has gifted you to do and what He has gifted you to do, He has called you to do."

2. . . . helps you know what God has _____ called you to do.

   The more we understand what we are *not* called to do, the easier it is to understand what we have been called to do. This understanding. . .

3. . . . relieves you from serving out of _____.

   When people serve out of "duty" they burn out and avoid ministry

4. . . . helps you understand how the Holy Spirit _____ you.

   1 Corinthians 3:9, **Your spiritual gift allows you to co-create with God, and . . .**

5. . . . fulfills a deep _____.

   God has placed in the souls of humankind, Christians and non-Christians alike, the need to serve others.

6. . . . builds _____ among _____.

   Understanding the gifts of others will help you see things from their perspective.

7. . . . equips you to fulfill God's _____ for you life.

   God has created each one of us with different gifts, talents, personalities, temperaments, and passions to outfit us to accomplish His unique purpose for each.

8. . . . adds to your self- _____.

   Real winners in life are those who accept themselves. Spiritual gifts allow individual believers to be themselves.

Note: Answers for each chapter's "For Group Discussion" questions can be found on pages 183-184

2

WHAT IS A SPIRITUAL GIFT?

*A practical look at how your spiritual gift relates
to the many areas of your life*

Everywhere I go I find Christians asking the question, "What is my spiritual gift?" When in reality they need to ask, "What is a spiritual gift?" You see, the problem is not that Christians don't know what *their* spiritual gifts are, the problem is that most Christians don't know what *a* spiritual gift is. They do not understand the *relationships* of spiritual gifts. They don't understand how a spiritual gift relates to their lives, how it relates to the lives of those people around them, how it relates to the local church or how it relates to the body of Christ as a whole. To give John J. Christian an additional name and make him John J. "Exhorter" Christian is only doing him an injustice.

Having a new name or title does not make you a better Christian or give you any more understanding of yourself or of those around you. Most contemporary material written on spiritual gifts does an adequate job of helping you recognize, discover, and determine what your spiritual gifts are. Also, many do a fine job of teaching about the individual members of the body. Unfortunately, however, few ever complete their teaching by assembling the body. Teaching a person only what *their* spiritual gift is without teaching them what *a* spiritual gift is would be like giving someone a new tool without giving them the operator's manual. They would never understand it fully nor be able to use it to its maximum potential. The same is true with spiritual gifts.

As a matter of fact, I discourage you from taking any spiritual gifts survey without also studying the principles that revolve around and relate to spiritual gifts. (That is why you should take the *Your Gifts* Spiritual Gifts Survey now—before reading any further—if you have not already.) These principles, combined with recognizing one's gifts, are proven to dramatically change lives *and* churches.

Close observation reveals nine identifying marks of a spiritual gift. An understanding of those characteristics will help you better understand how the spiritual gift you already have will help you serve the Lord more effectively:

1. ***Spiritual Gifts Are the Hands of God.*** In the courtyard of a quaint little church in a French village stood a beautiful marble statue of Jesus with outstretched hands. One day during World War II, a bomb struck near the statue and mutilated it. After the battle was over and the enemy had passed through, the citizens of the village decided to find the pieces of their beloved statue and reconstruct it. Though the statue was no work of art by Michelangelo or Bernini, it was a part of their lives and they cherished it. Even the scars on the body added to its beauty. But there was one problem. They were unable to find the hands of the statue. "A Christ without hands is not Christ at all," someone expressed in sorrow. "Hands with scars, yes. But what's a Lord without hands? We need a new statue."

   Then someone else came along with another idea, and it prevailed. A brass plaque was attached at the base of the statue that read, "I have no hands but your hands."

   Some years later someone saw that inscription and wrote the following lines:

   > *I have no hands but your hands to do my work today.*
   > *I have no feet but your feet to lead men on the way.*
   > *I have no tongue but your tongue to tell men how I died.*
   > *I have no help but your help to bring men to God's side.*

   A spiritual gift is the primary channel by which the Holy Spirit can minister through the believer. Spiritual gifts are God's provision for the Holy Spirit to minister to people, through people (1 Corinthians 12:25). Spiritual gifts allow us to serve as "God's hands."

Stop and consider the importance of this definition, for only through spiritual gifts can Christians minister to others with the *full* power of the Holy Spirit:

"The only hands God has are your hands."

One of the big obstacles in the church today is that we believe the church is supernatural in its origin, but not in its operation. When we experience a loss of power and effectiveness, it drives us to rely on human resources in an effort to correct the problem.

Early 20th century theologian and Dallas Theological Seminary founder Lewis Sperry Chafer writes, "The gift which is wrought by the Spirit is an expression of the Spirit's own ability rather than the mere use of human qualities in the one through whom He works."[1] Spiritual gifts are God's provision for the Holy Spirit to minister *through* the believer. The Holy Spirit uses these gifts to minister to you through other believers. The believer is not the source of ministry but only the instrument the Holy Spirit uses.

Remember, "The only hands God has are *your* hands."

2. A Spiritual Gift Is a Supernatural Capacity. A spiritual gift is also a *supernatural capacity* for service to God. Many authors writing about gifts use definitions like "a supernatural ability," "a God-given ability," "a Spirit-given ability," or "a divine ability." All definitions revolve around the word "ability." A spiritual gift is really not an "ability," but rather a "capacity" to develop an ability. The word "ability" has been confusing to many older Christians (referring to spiritual not physical age). Some mistakenly say, "I've been a Christian for years and I don't have any special 'ability' to do anything in the church; therefore, God must not have given me a gift." In reality, God has given every born-again believer at least one spiritual gift. (See "Who Has Spiritual Gifts?" in Chapter 4.)

Ability implies that you are able to do something, and a supernatural ability implies that you can do it supernaturally. A proper

23

distinction between "ability" and "capacity" is hard to make because descriptive words of both have somewhat the same meanings.

The real difference is this: an *ability* is a state of being, something that exists at the present, and a *capacity* enables for the future.

> A spiritual gift is a supernatural capacity, freely and graciously given by the sovereign God at the time of your salvation, enabling you to develop a supernatural ability.

The whole point is that if someone accepts Christ as Savior on Monday night and at the moment of salvation God gives him or her the gift of Teaching, the person would not automatically be a supernatural Teacher upon waking up Tuesday morning. Rather, he or she would wake up with the supernatural *capacity* (though it may be unknown to him or her at this point) to develop the supernatural *ability* of Teaching.

We must also distinguish between the gift of the Holy Spirit and the spiritual gifts. The gift of the Holy Spirit is given to the believer at conversion and manifests itself in the presence of the indwelling Spirit who constantly lives personally within the believer, empowering him or her for service. The spiritual gifts are also given at conversion. They manifest themselves as the tools of the Holy Spirit for carrying out the ministry of Christ through the individual believer, requiring the power of the indwelling Holy Spirit in order to be fully effective.

So then, a spiritual gift is a supernatural capacity, freely and graciously given by the sovereign God at the time of your salvation, enabling you to develop a supernatural ability, allowing the Holy Spirit to minister through you to your fellow humankind for the purpose of accomplishing His work.

3. *A Spiritual Gift Is a Supernatural Desire.* In 1 Timothy 3:1, Paul writes to Timothy saying, "This is a faithful saying, If a man desires the position of a bishop, he desires a good work" (KJV). In verse 2 he goes on to list the qualifications for a bishop. What is the very first qualification for a bishop? *Desire.* While Paul does not directly

address spiritual gifts in this passage, there is a principle to learn. His point is that before you can ever become an effective bishop, pastor or teacher, you must first have the desire.

When God gives you a spiritual gift, He also gives you a supernatural desire to perform the duties of that gift. For example, if He gives you the gift of Mercy-showing, He will give you a supernatural desire to comfort others. If Evangelism, He will give a supernatural desire to see many non-Christians won to Christ. As the believer grows and matures, this desire will grow stronger.

Channeled desire equals extraordinary success. Desire is the number one factor behind *all* accomplishment. If you study the lives of great and successful people, you will discover that a desire to achieve their objectives was the underlying ingredient for their success. But ordinary desire will not build much more than mediocrity. The supernatural desire given you with your spiritual gift starts small and is undeveloped; it alone will never build a champion for Christ. It takes what the secular "success teachers" call *a burning desire* or *passion,* and what the Bible calls a *burden.* Only a *burden* can do the extraordinary or drive a person to become a real champion for Christ.

The word *burden* has both a negative and positive connotation. In this context we speak of the positive meaning, "A motivating force from within that makes a demand on one's resources, whether material (see 1 Thessalonians 2:6) or spiritual (see Galatians 6:2, Revelation 2:24) or religious (see Acts 15:28) or emotional."[2] A *burden* is an insatiable hunger gnawing at your soul. It is a burning in your heart that drives you to do what God has called you to do. It's the passion that drives you and tugs at you from within to go that second mile.

If it takes this kind of passion to make an extraordinary champion, then how does someone get a burden? You must start with the desire given you with your spiritual gift and feed it and challenge it

25

with the reading, teaching, and preaching of God's Word. This will start your desire growing toward a burden and true passion. In other words, a *burden* will surface only after you have been either convicted by the Holy Spirit through the preaching of the Word or taken part in practical how-to training in the area that appeals to *your passion*. A spiritual gift can be compared to a muscle: You have many muscles in your body; the more you use them the stronger they become. With exercise like weight lifting, the muscles will increase in size and definition—they become more noticeable. With lack of use, muscles shrink and weaken. Likewise, a spiritual gift will become stronger and more noticeable as you exercise it. If you don't use it, it stays or becomes small and weak.

4. *Spiritual Gifts Are the Tools for Doing the Work of the Ministry.*
Spiritual gifts are the tools for building the church. Ephesians 4:12 says gifts are given "for the perfecting of the saints, for the work of the ministry, for the edifying of the body of Christ" (KJV).

Many Christians know the tools God has given them, but they don't know what they're to be used for—"Should I dig a hole with it, or saw a board, or maybe mix cement with it?" How can we do the work of the ministry properly if we don't recognize which tools we have and how to use them?

This would be like taking an indigenous hunter out of the Amazon jungle, giving him a box of tools and sending him out to build a house. If no one showed him the purpose of each tool and how to use it, it is very doubtful he would ever get the job done. If he were committed and determined to overcome his frustrations, mistakes and failures, however, he might get the house built; although, I think many of us would not want to buy it.

Here's one thing for certain: we need to learn how to recognize and use the tools God has given each of us. It will make us more effective. You see, God will never give you a hammer and ask you to saw a board, nor will He give you a saw and ask you to drive nails.

On the contrary, if God wants you to cut boards, He will give you a saw, and if He wants you to drive nails, He will give you a hammer. Therefore, when you recognize your gift, you must determine how to use it to be effective in ministry and how your gift can contribute to the TEAM—your church.

5. *A Spiritual Gift Is the Source of Joy in Your Christian Life.* When someone gives you an earthly gift, such as for your birthday or at Christmas, you receive the gift with joy. However, the greatest joy comes when you are able to use that gift in some part of your life. For example, when a woman receives gloves from a friend, she receives the greatest amount of joy when wearing them with a special outfit or to keep warm in winter as she remembers the person's friendship. So it is with the spiritual gifts. We receive them with joy, but the greatest joy comes with using them to minister for the glory of God.

You must start with the desire given you with your spiritual gift and feed it and challenge it with the reading, teaching, and preaching of God's Word.

There is no other way you can be as fulfilled as when you are using your God-given spiritual gifts.

Several Greek words in the New Testament are translated "gift" or "spiritual gift." Let's examine them:

1. *Doma*: Luke 11:13, Ephesians 4:8. The word means "a present, to build, a gift."[3]

2. (a) *Charisma:* Romans 12:6, 1 Corinthians 12:4, 9, 28, 30, 31. If I were to ask you if you were charismatic, you may answer, "No." But, the truth is, all Christians are charismatic. Because of the movement's emphasis on spiritual gifts, the Charismatic Movement simply derived its name from the word *charisma* (the most common Greek word translated "spiritual gifts" in Scriptures). The word means, "A (divine) gratuity, a (spiritual) endowment, a religious qualification, a (free) gift."[4] The word *charisma* is a form of the Greek word *charis*.

27

(b) *Charis*: In most instances when *charis* appears in the New Testament it can be interpreted "grace," meaning unmerited favor. The root word of both of these words is the Greek word *char*.

(c) *Char.* This word means joy, happiness or fulfillment.

The basic idea taught through this original word usage is summed up by the authors of the *Liberty Commentary*: "As you use the gift which God gave you by His grace, it produces the greatest amount of joy or fulfillment, spiritually, in your life."5 They go on to say, "Your spiritual gift is the source of joy in your Christian life. When you are using your given gift, you will be able to function with *maximum fulfillment* and *minimum frustration*. Using your gift for the service of Christ is the only way you can fulfill that God-given inner need to serve others."

Every Christian should have a "personal ministry." Your personal ministry should reflect your spiritual gift or at least allow it to be manifest. What is a "personal ministry?" That which you do for God that benefits someone else.

6. *A Spiritual Gift Is a Divine Motivator.* Motivation is possibly the greatest single contribution to understanding the function and application of spiritual gifts, because it recognizes that spiritual gifts are not just a title God gives to the believer, but a major motivating factor in the lives of recipients. It recognizes that spiritual gifts have a definite influence on our being. Motivation gives a person energy and a willingness to sacrifice. It gives us the supernatural drive to go that second mile. When we are working in areas of ministry that complement our gifts we are willing to work harder, stay longer, and pay more to see success.

Your personal ministry should reflect your spiritual gift or at least allow it to be manifest.

Many books are written on the subject of motivation. They all say practically the same thing: "*You* can't motivate any one other than yourself, because motivation comes from within." One writer summed it up best saying something like this, "The best possible way to motivate people to a task is to find people who are already motivated." If you plan to motivate them yourself, you might find such a statement discouraging, especially if no one around you is motivated.

But the good news is that every Christian *is already* motivated, in the sense that every Christian has a spiritual gift. Along with that spiritual gift comes a divine, supernatural, internal motivation from God to perform the responsibilities of the gift. That capacity and supernatural desire becomes the motivator and causes actions to take place without the necessity of outside motivation and prompting. In fact, the Holy Spirit actually does the motivating from *within* the person.

7. *A Spiritual Gift Divinely Influences Motives or Reasons for Our Behavior.* Suppose you had just bought your brand-new dream car. You had dreamed about having such a car all your life. You saved, invested, and sacrificed so that you could finally buy the car of your dreams. As you drive home from the dealership in your pride and joy, you pass a little boy on the side of the road. He is poised with a rock in his hand as if to throw it toward your new car. You cringe as you see a nightmare coming true. The little boy fires the dreaded missile into the passenger side door of your new dream car. As the rock finds purchase, you slam on the brakes, skid to a stop, and jump out of the car. Feeling the anger overtaking your entire being, you head for the little scrounge asking yourself what the penalty is for murdering the 5-year-old who just shattered your dream.

Before you can say anything, however, the little boy cries and says, "I'm sorry I dented your car, but my little brother broke his leg and that's the only way I could get a car to stop." Suddenly, your motives have changed from anger to understanding and a

29

willingness to help. Such is the case with our motives for serving God and helping others. We can understand why people behave or think the way they do when we understand their spiritual gifts.

As we learn the characteristics, strengths, and weaknesses of each gift, we can see others—even our families—in a different light.

As we learn the characteristics, strengths, and weaknesses of each gift, we can see others—even our families—in a different light.

Several years ago I was on vacation with my family at a national theme park. The bright sun was really bothering my eyes, as I had left my sunglasses in the car. Since it would have taken at least an hour to retrieve them, I decided to buy another pair. I found a rack that must have had a hundred pairs on it. They were all the identical style, but were in every color of the rainbow. There was red, pink, blue, green, yellow, orange, and so on. I found it impossible to just pick out a pair and purchase them. I had to try on every different color first. I put on the red pair and looked all around and my whole world was tinted red. Whatever color I was looking through was the color that was influencing my vision.

Your spiritual gift is the same way. When you "put on" the gift of Teaching, you look at the world through the eyes of a Teacher. When you put on the gift of Giving, you look at the world through the eyes of a Giver. When you put on the gift of Serving, you look at the world through the eyes of a Server, and so on. Your gift influences how to see your environment. When you understand this in yourself and in others, you'll realize that a lot of those people you think are being difficult, aren't—they are just looking at the situation from a different perspective . . . a gift-influenced perspective.

There would be fewer church squabbles if more Christians understood what motivates people who have gifts that differ from their own.

8. A Spiritual Gift Is a Divine Calling and Divine Responsibility.

Have you ever heard or sung the song *I'm in the Lord's Army* at church or summer camp? Adults have heard "You're in the Lord's Army" preached and during the invitation heard the question, "Will you volunteer for the Lord's Army?" A stirring invitation? Yes. A way to get commitments? Maybe. Good theology? No! The Lord's Army *is not* a volunteer army. The question is not, "Will you volunteer for the Lord's Army?" The question is, "Are you a draft dodger or not?" If you are a Christian, you *are* in His Army whether you want to be or not (see Acts 1:8, Ephesians 2:10). God has equipped you for battle (your spiritual gift), and you have a divine responsibility to use that gift.

Note that Ephesians 4:1 is Paul's introduction to the subject of spiritual gifts. He said, "As a prisoner for the Lord, then, I urge you to live a life worthy of the calling you have received." And in verse 11, he lists the principles concerning spiritual gifts. The important thing to notice is that when Paul starts talking about spiritual gifts he begins by talking about your calling or vocation.

I have seen many gifts lists where an asterisk (*) is put by several gifts and at the bottom of the page the author writes something like, "This gift may require a calling from God." The truth is, *all* gifts require a calling from God, and with each one comes an automatic calling. *What God has gifted you to do, He has called you to do, and what He has called you to do, He has gifted you to do.* When He gives you the gift, He gives you the responsibility to use it. Every believer has been called into full-time service; however, not every Christian has been called to make that service their occupation or means of support.

If you are a Christian, you are in His Army whether you want to be or not.

Another passage speaking of the responsibility that comes with your spiritual gift is 1 Peter 4:10: "Each of you should use whatever gift you have received to serve others, as faithful stewards of God's grace in its various forms." This passage speaks of spiritual gifts in a more general sense than the other passages.

31

Nevertheless, Peter *is* speaking of spiritual gifts in the light of stewardship. A steward is one who is entrusted with and held accountable for something that belongs to his master.

Every believer has been called into full-time service; however, not every Christian has been called to make that service their occupation or means of support.

In Matthew 25:14-30, we study the parable of the talents. The talents mentioned here are not natural talents, spiritual gifts or any type of ability. These talents refer to a very large denomination of money. We can, however, still gain the biblical principle of accountability from this passage. "For the kingdom of heaven is as a man traveling to a far country, who called his own servants, and delivered unto them his goods. And unto one he gave five talents, to another two, and to another one: to every man according to his several ability" (Matthew 25:14-15, KJV). Today the word *several* is best interpreted as *capacity;* therefore, the verse is saying, "according to the capacity of his ability."

For example, you may have the gift of Shepherding with the capacity to shepherd 5,000 people. Therefore, God will allow you to exercise your gift according to that capacity and hold you accountable for it at that level. Another Christian may have the same gift but only have the capacity to shepherd 20 people. In God's eyes, the latter is no less. This is the capacity for which God will hold that person accountable. You are accountable for the capacity as well as the gift. Think of your gift as a bucket and the contents of the bucket as its capacity. God may give some people a ten-gallon bucket while He gives others a one-gallon bucket.

The parable goes on to say that when the master returned home, the servant to whom he had given five talents had doubled them and gave his master back ten. The servant who had two talents had also doubled his. The master replied, "Well done, good and faithful servant! You have been faithful with a few things; I will put you in charge of many things. Come and share your master's happiness!"

(Matthew 25:21). But the servant who had the one talent had taken it and buried it. He was a poor steward, as he had not properly used that which his master had entrusted to him.

At this point you may want to consider the question: when you have the opportunity to stand before Christ at the Judgment, what will He say to you? Will He say, "Well done, good and faithful servant," or might He say, as He did to the third servant in verse 26, "You wicked, lazy servant!" The Bible plainly states, "For we must *all* appear before the judgment seat of Christ, so that each of us may receive what is due us for the things done while in the body, whether good or bad" (2 Corinthians 5:10, *emphasis mine*).

9. *Spiritual Gifts Are the Building Blocks of the Church.* In his book on witnessing, David Innes talks about his first church. He admits to being too program-centered, even though people came to Christ and the church grew. He says:

33

"I started with the programs and not the people. Eventually, I began to dry up. Instead of starting with the people's needs and designing programs, ministry, teaching, etc., to fit into and meet their needs, I always started with the programs and tried to get people to fit into those programs. For some, the programs happened to meet their needs. For many, they didn't and these people were left out.

"I even quoted Bible verses to support my programs and get people to do what I wanted them to do. If I were there today as pastor, I would start with the people first, find out exactly what their needs were and design all programs, teaching and preaching to meet their needs and not mine, being people centered rather than being program centered. *The New Testament is all but silent on methodology and is remarkably free of programs,*" he observed.[6]

A church should be built with people instead of programs. There is nothing wrong with programs—they are simply an organized means to reach an objective. Many churches, however, build super organizations and super programs and try to fit their people into them. What we need to do is start with people and their gifts, with their motivations, passions, and abilities, and build the church with them.

> *What we need to do is start with the people and their gifts, with their motivations, passions, and abilities, and build the church with them.*

Someone once said, "Never use a great people to build a great church, but use a great church to build a great people." On the contrary we *should* use a great people to build a great church and then use a great church to meet the needs of a great people. It is an unending cycle—people ministering to people through the living organism called the church.

The world even agrees with the philosophy of building with people first. Management teachers and writers today emphasize this philosophy, saying, "The key to make man effective is to start with the person, find out what his strengths are, and put him in a position where he can make full use of his strengths. Never start with the job and make the man fit into the job or the program. Start with the man and make the job or the program fit into his strengths. This will automatically minimize and render harmless his weaknesses. This is being people centered in leadership."7 Business is the same as the church: you need to build with the means not the task.

Now and then I am challenged with, "Didn't Jesus say, 'I will build my church'?" (see Matthew 16:18). Yes, He did, and 1 Corinthians 3:9 says, "For we are co-workers in God's service; you are God's field, God's building." Christ *will* build His church, but He's going to do it through you. Chuck Millhuff says it nicely, "God can, if I will."

34

NEXT STEPS

A spiritual gift is not just a superficial name we add to a believer once he or she is saved. A spiritual gift is something that takes hold of a believer and manifests itself through his or her life. Understanding our spiritual gifts removes the frustration and confusion from serving God. When someone learns the definition of what *a* gift is, he or she realizes that it is not just another characteristic of the Spirit-filled life, but it is *the* way the Spirit-filled life manifests itself. What the Spirit-filled life is all about is for the believer to take the area where God has equipped him or her and put it into service for God.

> *Understanding our spiritual gifts removes the frustration and confusion from serving God.*

Regardless of what gift is present in a believer's life, it has certain affects on his or her life. The gift strongly influences the desires and motives of living and ministry. Each gift has characteristics that can influence a person's motives both for good and bad. Because gifts are such a strong part of motives, we can truthfully say that when Christians are miserable in their area of service, chances are they are not exercising their God-given spiritual gifts.

People are motivated to action for two reasons: either they *have to* or they *want to*. Spiritual gifts are the "want to" of Christian service.

35

FOR PERSONAL REFLECTION

1. How does a "capacity" differ from a talent or ability?

2. Who belongs in the "Lord's Army"? How has God equipped His army?

3. If God has given you a gift, what else has He done?

4. What unusually strong desire has God given you to do in His work? Which spiritual gift does that correspond with? If you have that spiritual gift, how do you develop it?

5. Discuss a situation that has arisen in your life that changed your motives?

6. How important are motives to actions? Can you determine another person's motives by their actions?

FOR GROUP DISCUSSION

Everybody wants to know their spiritual gifts. The problem is *not* that Christians do not know what *their* spiritual gifts are; the problem is that most Christians don't know what *a* spiritual gift is.

1. **Spiritual gifts are the _____ of _____.**

   Spiritual gifts allow the Holy Spirit to minister to others, through us.

2. **A spiritual gift is a supernatural _____.**

   A. Not an ability: enabling the present.

   B. Capacity: enabling for the future.

3. **Spiritual gifts are the _____ for doing the work of the ministry.**

   Ephesians 4:11-12

4. **A spiritual gift is the _____ of _____**

   in your Christian life.

   A. *Charisma* – a divine gratuity, a spiritual endowment, a free gift. A form of *Charis*.

   B. *Charis* – usually translated "grace." Root word is *Char*.

   C. *Char* – joy, happiness, fulfillment.

5. **A spiritual gift is a supernatural _____.**

   1 Timothy 3:1 – the first requirement for service.

6. **A spiritual gift is a divine _____.**

7. **A spiritual gift divinely influences your _____**

   or _____ for doing things.

8. **A spiritual gift is a divine _____and responsibility.**

   Ephesians 4:1

Note: Answers for each chapter's "For Group Discussion" questions can be found on pages 183-184

3

SPIRITUAL GIFTS AND THEIR RELATIONSHIP TO GOD'S WILL

Whenever a handful of Christians get together, it is only a matter of time until someone brings up the subject of *God's will*. As Christians, we all have great concern about God's will. We want to know whom to marry, where to live, where to go to church. We wonder what kind of car or home God wants us to buy. How many children should we have? Unfortunately, no verses say, "Thou shalt have six children," or "Thou shalt drive a Ford," or "Thou shalt remain single," or "Thou shalt (whatever it is we want an easy answer to)." Yet these are subjects that greatly concern us. Many of us will spend much of our lives seeking such answers, and questioning decisions on issues simpler than these—issues for which there are no clear and direct answers in Scripture.

We are rightfully concerned about wrong turns. For instance, it is said that in the United States alone there are more than 23,000 ways to make a living. According to some surveys, approximately eighty-eight percent of Americans who work have jobs they do not like or they would not choose for a career. Christians should not be included in such statistics, for we have a God who can lead us in the paths best suited to us. If that is true, how do we find God's will or direction for life?

Interestingly, two of the major passages Paul writes concerning spiritual gifts begin by talking about God's will. In Romans 12:2, Paul's introduction to spiritual gifts speaks of that "good, acceptable, and perfect will of God" (KJV). So, if we want to know what is that good, acceptable, and perfect will of God for our lives, then it must have something to do with spiritual gifts. However, to only address the relationship of spiritual gifts to God's will would be a mistake. It is necessary to address a complete overview of God's will in order to understand how spiritual gifts relate to it.

Many good books have been written on the subject of God's will, but many will unintentionally mislead you. So let's start off by addressing what may be confusing.

GOD'S WILL FOR YOUR LIFE IS NOT BAD

Many Christians fear God's will. The late Ray Stedman says in his classic book, *Body Life*, "Somewhere the idea has found deep entrenchment in Christian circles that doing what God wants you to do is always unpleasant; Christians must always make choices between doing what they want to do and being happy, and doing what God wants them to do and being completely miserable."1 Nothing could be further from the truth. Many Christians think that if they give in to God's will, God will strip them naked, take everything they own, give them a loincloth and send them to Africa. After all, isn't that God's calling to everybody—to be a missionary?

Have you ever heard it said, "Don't say that, or that's just what God will make you do," as if God were looking for ways to torment you? God is our loving Father and He wants only the best for His children. He is not going to put us in any situation that will compromise our effectiveness to serve Him. That would be contrary to God's nature.

> Many Christians think that if they give in to God's will, God will strip them naked, take everything they own, give them a loincloth and send them to Africa.

Why can we justify looking at God's will for His children being bad while His will for the unbeliever is to provide deliverance from sin, oppression and judgment? Galatians 1:4 says, ". . . who gave himself for our sins to rescue us from the present evil age, according to the will of our God and Father . . . "God is not willing to deliver us from "this present evil age" in order to place us back into misery. Part of the deliverance we receive through Christ is deliverance from things that make us miserable.

One pastor, after studying spiritual gifts and the will of God, said, "A great surprise in my life was to discover God's will would make me happy."

GOD'S WILL FOR YOUR LIFE IS NOT FIXED

"One of the most amazing and practical truths of the Bible is that God has a definite plan for your life." "God has a blueprint for your life." "God's will is like a road map with your trip laid out for you." These are statements taken from various introductions of materials written on God's will. "A definite plan," "A blueprint," "A planned trip"; such terminology can confuse and discourage you.

The good news is that God has many provisions in His will for our failures and shortcomings.

The voice of discouragement says, "I am 39 years old (or whatever number) and just finding out that God has a definite plan for my life. Surely, I have blown it many times by now. My blueprint does not even resemble the original structure that God had planned, so why even bother with it now? I am bound to arrive at a different destination than God originally planned."

Many Christians have married unsaved mates only to discover, years later, it was not God's will for them. Now, some want to "trade in" their mate, which is not God's will either. The point is, we have all made many mistakes along the way and the idea that God's will is non-bendable, fixed or non-variable can put undue pressure on us.

The good news is that God has many provisions in His will for our failures and shortcomings. You haven't missed the boat; he has even allowed you the privilege of making some decisions and choices while remaining in His will.

A study of the Scriptures which speak of God's will clearly reveals that God's specific will deals with spiritual qualities and the spiritual condition of believers rather than a deed or specific place of service or task.

GOD'S WILL FOR YOUR LIFE IS NOT LOST

Many books and messages include remarks like, "How to find the will of God," "Seeking God's will," or "Searching for God's will," as if it were lost. They leave us wandering aimlessly through life until we can stumble upon God's will. There is nothing to find or discover, instead there is something we need to recognize. I do not condemn the use of the terms. They are commonly used; however, we do need to realize that we can confuse ourselves with them.

39

God's will is easy to recognize in Scripture. Psalm 40:8 says, "I desire to do your will, my God; your law *is* within my heart." In various translations of this passage, the word "is" runs in italics. This means the translator added it to help us better understand the passage. Read it without the word "is." Right! Now we see "your will" and "your law" are one and the same. They are both within our hearts. In fact, it could say, "Your will is your law within my heart."

The exciting news is that *as a believer, God's will for your life is part of your very being.* We do not have to discover it or find it at all! What we need to do is learn to *recognize* what is already there.

GOD'S WILL FOR YOU IS NOT REVEALED TO OTHERS

Isn't it funny that when the subject of God's will is brought up, how much other people know about God's will for *your* life? They have advice as to just what God wants you to do, yet in many cases they are very confused as to what God's will is for their own lives. God will reveal His will for your life to *you,* not to someone else.

Several years ago, my wife and I were "searching" for God's will for our lives. We visited a Christian missions center in Pennsylvania. We spent a lot of time with their counselors. We were very confused since at that time we had no idea what God's will was for our lives. But also, there was no doubt *they knew* God's will for our lives. They were certain God had called us to missions and we were resisting God's will by not accepting the call.

The exciting news is that as a believer, God's will for your life is part of your very being. We do not have to discover it or find it at all!

At that point we made a decision to go elsewhere to a school and pursue a course of study that had nothing to do with missions. Our present plans still have nothing to do with missions in the traditional sense of the word, and we have never doubted that we made the right decision. My wife and I are totally convinced that we are in God's will. Yet, when we left that center, the people there were saying that we were refusing to accept or do God's will.

Legitimate counsel where someone shares principles from the Word of God will help you make decisions based on God's will. (Hopefully this chapter is doing some of that.) Young people can receive such counsel from Christian parents. However, some people are always imposing God's will for *their* life on *your* life. The principle to learn is: *God will reveal His will for your life to* you. You will have to make the final decision.

In the case of a married couple, God will reveal it to both; He will never divide a couple.

GOD'S WILL IS NOT BASED ON CIRCUMSTANCES

In Judges 6:37-40 we read the story of Gideon and the fleece. From this story we have gleaned a popular phrase in discerning God's will—"putting out the fleece." If you will recall the story, Gideon laid out a wool fleece on his threshing floor, and asked God to fill the fleece with dew—while keeping the ground around it dry—as a sign of God's confirmation. And that is what happened.

Today when we "put out the fleece," we sometimes wrongly set up circumstances and ask God to fit them. We say, "If you want me to do that, God, then You must do this."

Decisions based on circumstances in your life rest upon your having a large amount of faith. Some Christians can make life-altering decisions based on circumstances, but *most Christians cannot.* Most Christians have not developed the faith it takes to make these big decisions.

Too many Christians would be like the elderly Scottish lady who went to country homes to sell thread, buttons and shoe strings. When she came to unmarked crossroads, she threw a stick into the air to determine which road to take that day. Observed throwing the stick into the air several times one day, she was asked why. She replied, "It has pointed every time to the road going to the right, and I want to go on the road to the left. It looks smoother." She kept throwing the stick until it pointed the direction she wanted to go. This principle of "putting out the fleece" and using circumstances should not be used this way, of course.

41

Some people are always imposing God's will for their life on your life. The principle to learn is: God will reveal His will for your life to you.

We usually use circumstances for major decisions and trust in our own intelligence to make little decisions. When a big decision comes up, we "put out the fleece" and, in most cases, it does not work. In some cases it may work, so I do not entirely discard this principle.

GOD'S WILL IS NOT CONTRARY TO GOD'S WORD

"Lord, You know I am out of work and have been out for a long time. The bills are piling up. We don't have money to buy groceries. The children don't have shoes. Father, is it Your will that I rob the convenience store on the corner so we will have money to take care of our financial needs?" This is a foolish prayer because it is contrary to God's Word, which says, "You shall not steal" (Exodus 20:15). That might be an extreme example because it is obvious you would not pray about being a thief. But there are principles in the Bible that we should use in determining God's will.

A Christian may wish to marry a non-Christian because they're in love. But 2 Corinthians 6:14 says, "Do not be yoked together with unbelievers." Therefore, this cannot be God's will.

The main principle is: *anything that is contrary to God's Word is also contrary to God's will.*

To summarize: If we cannot rely on the previous "Nots" to help us recognize God's will for our lives, then where can we look? In God's Word—the Bible. So let's look to see what God's Word says is God's will for your life.

GOD'S WILL IS . . . [2]
God's Will for Your Life Is That You Be *Saved*

Look at 2 Peter 3:9, "The Lord is not slow in keeping his promise, as some understand slowness. Instead he is patient with you, not wanting anyone to perish, but everyone to come to repentance." Therefore, God's will for your life is for you to be saved; He is not willing that any person should die and go to hell. Romans 8:7-8 says, "The mind governed by the flesh is hostile to God; it does not submit to God's law, nor can it do so. Those who are in the realm of the flesh cannot please God." This might be a simple statement to make, but if a person is not saved, they are not in God's will.

God's Will for Your Life Is That You Be *Sanctified*

First Thessalonians 4:3-4 says, "It is God's will that you should be sanctified: that you should avoid sexual immorality; that each of you should learn to control your own body in a way that is holy and honorable." Sanctification means to make holy, pure, set apart. As you read forward in this passage, you will see God intends for you to be holy or set apart. You are to abstain from fornication; that means to remain pure. You are to be controlled by the Spirit, not the flesh. You are not to defraud your brother. God's will for your life is that you be sanctified.

God's Will for Your Life Is That You Be *Spirit-filled*

Ephesians 5:17-18 says, "Therefore do not be foolish, but understand what the Lord's will is. Do not get drunk on wine, which leads to debauchery. Instead, be filled with the Spirit." To be filled with the Spirit means to be controlled by the Spirit. Verse 18 is an excellent verse to exemplify this. Paul uses it to show us what being controlled by the Spirit is. He says, "Do not get drunk on wine." Have you ever seen anyone drunk, full of wine, walking down the street? He has a hard time walking because the wine that fills him has total control of his body. The same is true with the Holy Spirit. When you are filled with the Spirit, then the Spirit will have control of you.

God's Will for Your Life Is That You Be *Submissive*

First Peter 2:13-15 says, "Submit yourselves for the Lord's sake to every human authority: whether to the emperor, as the supreme authority, or to governors, who are sent by him to punish those who do wrong and to commend those who do right. For it is God's will that by doing good you should silence the ignorant talk of foolish people." This passage indicates that we are subject to those God has put in authority over us. We are to be subject to God, to our pastor, to our civil leaders, to the police. Why should we be subject to these people? (In many cases we are talking about being subject to non-Christians.) The Scripture says that we "should silence the ignorant talk of foolish (e.g. unsaved) people." We should not have a rebellious spirit, which is one of the first things someone will spot in you.

One pastor states, "We are training leaders at our school and you will never become a good leader until you can become a good follower."

You might say, "That doesn't pertain to me, because God hasn't called me to be a leader." But on the contrary, God has called us all to be leaders. We need to be outstanding as leaders in the eyes of the non-Christian world. We all have that responsibility to help lead every one of those people to the saving knowledge of Jesus Christ. At one time or another, we all have leadership roles.

One of the biggest areas where Christians do not submit themselves to civil leaders is simply obeying the speed limit. If we are guilty of speeding, we show our children and others around us that we don't think we have to submit to the laws. Thus, we send the message that we believe the laws are unfair or unjust, and that we have valid reasons to violate them. God's will for our lives is that we be submissive.

God's Will for Your Life Is That You *Suffer*

First Peter 4:19 states, "So then, those who suffer according to God's will should commit themselves to their faithful Creator and continue to do good." Relatedly, look at 1 Peter 3:17, "For it is better, if it is God's will, to suffer for doing good than for doing evil." Many of you are thinking, "Boy! Do I qualify for this one." But look again at the passage, it says for "doing good." Most of our suffering is not for doing good but for improper or wrong doings. As I look back over my life, I can see times that I suffered both physically, financially, and emotionally. But if I am truthful, most of the time it was for "evil doing" or ignorance, or violation of scriptural principles that God has laid down for me. By violating them, I in turn suffered.

Of course, we live in a fallen world, and terrible things happen to good people all the time, of no fault of their own. I am not trying to minimize the wounds that you may carry from past abuses, tragedies, or wrongs committed against you, but to point out that even if you have been victimized or traumatized, God wants to heal you, restore you, and unleash your gifts and potential.

There are many levels in this area of suffering. We think of Christians having to suffer in religiously repressive or totalitarian nations where they cannot gather to worship, and where many have been beaten or put to death for their faith in Jesus Christ. This is what we think of as suffering. Thank God if you are living in a free country where you can share your faith and do not have to suffer as some other Christians do. But the truth is, many Christians will suffer if they are willing to live an obedient life. Many Christians will suffer if they are willing to take a stand or live by the principles that are laid down in the Scriptures.

Many business people suffer because the rules governing business today are no longer based on Judeo-Christian ethics. In a lot of businesses the motto is "get all you can, can all you get" or "do it any way possible." Many Christian business people bid on jobs knowing if they don't bend a little rule or if they stay in line scripturally, they have no chance of getting the job. But if they just twist the rules a little bit and do something that is acceptable in the business world, they can get the order. Yet they know in their hearts Christ will convict them. The Christian businessperson who takes a stand will often lose his work to com-

But the truth is, many Christians will suffer if they are willing to live an obedient life.

petitors. The executive who doesn't follow the board's directive for ethical reasons makes business harder on herself. She suffers.

The question is, "Why should we suffer?" Let's look at 1 Peter 2:21, "To this you were called, because Christ suffered for you, leaving you an example, that you should follow in his steps." God's will for your life is that you suffer.

God's Will for Your Life Is That You *Serve*

In Romans 12:1-3 Paul writes, "Therefore, I urge you, brothers and sisters, in view of God's mercy, to offer your bodies as a living sacrifice, holy and pleasing to God—this is your true and proper worship. Do not conform to the pattern of this world, but be transformed by the renewing of your mind. Then you will be able to test and approve what God's will is—his good, pleasing and perfect will."

This is the most commonly used passage in most material that addresses God's will. Bible commentaries offer a variety of interpretations of what this passage means. Many commentaries, however, have this passage backwards. To clarify what I am saying, there is an old rule of thumb about working with the book of Romans: if you discover what the "therefore" is "there for" you will understand the passage. The passage of Romans 12:1 starts off, "*Therefore*, I urge you."

Using the "therefore" rule you have to look backward to see what Paul is talking about. And in this case, he has been talking about the goodness (mercies) of God. Now he is saying, "Therefore, based on the goodness of God, you need to be in service. You need to make your bodies a living sacrifice (in contrast to the dead sacrifices of the Old Testament) and be in service to God. Now, I am going to tell you how to do it and what you have to do it with." This is his introduction to spiritual gifts.

There is an old rule of thumb about working with the book of Romans: if you discover what the "therefore" is "there for" you will understand the passage.

Paul is basically saying, "If you are going to be in that good, acceptable and perfect will of God, you will have to use your spiritual gifts." Paul is now giving you the practical application based on the previous chapters of doctrine. He is saying, "If you are going to serve God in a task-oriented way, in a way that you will accomplish something with your life, in a way that you will accomplish something for God, here is the practical way to fulfill the doctrine that I have been teaching you."

In a parallel passage, Ephesians 4:1, Paul starts off, "I therefore, the prisoner of the Lord, beseech you that ye walk worthy of the vocation wherewith ye are called" (KJV). Again, it is interesting to see that "the vocation wherewith ye are called" is referring to a calling for your life, God's will for your life. In another passage, 1 Peter 4:10, Peter states, "As each one has received a *special* gift, *employ it in serving one another* as good stewards of the manifold grace of God" (second emphasis mine). These Scriptures talk about service. Service is making your body a living sacrifice, doing something with your body.

In summary of our first six principles, Romans 12 is a capstone passage for the other five principles that we have looked at: saved, sanctified, Spirit-filled, submissive, and suffering. It is a kind of summary statement of all of the others, because when you are doing all these other five principles you are making your body a living sacrifice. Paul says your reasonable service is a living sacrifice for service to Christ. God's will for your life is that you serve.

At this point you may say, "These are six pretty good principles, but you have not answered the question that is tormenting me about God's will. I can understand that these things are revealed in the Word of God as being His will for my life. I understand that part of God's will for my life, but what I need is to find a means of determining the unrevealed things. These principles you

46

covered are all revealed in the Word of God. There are a lot of decisions I need to make that are not addressed directly in the Word of God."

Let me bring out a different principle. **God will never reveal to you His unrevealed will if you are not willing to do His revealed will.** A man might say, "I know that God's will for my life is for me not to smoke, but what I really need to know is should we make this move that is coming up?" Or, "I know God's will for my life is that I don't lose my temper, but what I really need to know is how do I make this other decision in my life?" Well, that leads us right into the seventh and last principle by asking, "What is God's will for my life?"

GOD'S WILL FOR YOUR LIFE IS . . .

I shared with you earlier about the mission center and how pressure was put on my wife and me to go on the mission field. We even got to the point where we did a little bit of arguing and some debating. Real pressure was put on us when one of the counselors finally put me on the spot by asking, "How can you be so positive that God doesn't want you to go into missions?" Without thinking or understanding I blurted out what I would later discover to be a very important principle in determining God's will and decision-making.

47

I said, "Because I don't want to!" This brings us to the last principle. Very seldom will you hear this principle taught, and undoubtedly it's because it can be so easily misused. I didn't begin teaching the will of God with principle number seven because it could be very misleading when taken out of context.

I understand the danger of this principle. Therefore, I want to emphasize very strongly that *if* you are *saved*, *if* you are *sanctified*, *if* you are *Spirit-filled*, *if* you are *submissive*, *if* you are *suffering*, and *if* you are *serving*, then, and only then, God's will for your life is *whatever you desire*.

That's right, God's will for your life is whatever you desire, whatever you want. If, at this point, you meet all of these qualifications: saved, sanctified, Spirit-filled, submissive, suffering and serving, then who do you think is controlling your desires? Who do you think is controlling your wants? It is impossible for anyone to faithfully practice these six principles and then do things that are undesirable in the sight of God.

God's will is whatever you desire. Psalm 37:4 says, "Delight thyself also in the Lord: and he shall give thee the desires of thine heart"(KJV). It is not saying He will give you all the material things you desire. It is saying He will give you the *desires* themselves; He will place the *desires* in your heart.

Where should you go to school? Where should you live? What church should you attend? Where should you send your children to school? Wherever you want to. Whatever you want to do. If you are living these principles, then your desire will be God's will for your life because God will put those desires in your heart. He will let you use your innermost feelings to direct your path.

"But," comes the argument, "Proverbs 3:6 says, 'He (not we) will make your paths straight.' " Let's be realistic for a minute. God doesn't write on the wall with His finger any more and the U.S. Postal Service doesn't extend to Heaven; nor can we get direction from super-bass voices from above as in the movies. Without these, we rely on the Word of God and the Spirit of God. The Spirit indwells us and influences our innermost being. If God wills that you do something contrary to your desire, He will simply change your desire (see Philippians 2:13).

I know that in my own experience, the men at the mission center thought my wife and I were being rebellious and not willing to accept God's will for our lives. Now, years later, I can look back and say, "I know that we made the right decision," because God has blessed us and there is no doubt in our minds we are in His will.

This brings us to an important observation. You and I are not living these first six principles to perfection. But, the closer we come to living these principles of being saved, sanctified, Spirit-filled, submissive, suffering, and serving, the more pleasing our "desire-based" decisions will be to God. The more we neglect and stray from the six principles, the less accurate our desire-based decisions will be.

Remember that *serving* is one of the six principles. The importance of serving in relation to desire-based decisions is evident in Proverbs 16:3: "Commit to the Lord whatever you do, and he will establish your plans."

TEST YOUR DESIRES

You must be able to distinguish between *desires* and *whims.* Impulsive decisions, even in the name of God, can play havoc with your life.

Many advertisers rely on what they call "point of purchase" advertising or, in other words, "whim purchasing." Rarely is an item purchased on a whim a necessity. That is why advertisers use this form of marketing. They know you won't buy it if you think about it. The same is true of decisions made on whims; if you think about it and pray about it your decision may be different.

Test your desires to see if they are whims. There are basically two tests: *time* and *knowledge.* Whims will seldom stand the test of time. Yet, God-given desires will grow with time. Also weigh your desires against God's Word; God does not put desires that clash with biblical principles or truths in your heart.

THE SOURCE OF YOUR PASSIONS

So, what is the relationship between God's will and spiritual gifts? First, your gift is always in perfect harmony with God's will for your life. Remember, *what God has called you to do He has gifted you to do, and what He has gifted you to do, He has called you to do.* Second, understanding God's will for your life is much easier when you know your spiritual gift. The earlier you understand your spiritual gift, the easier it will be to determine God's will for your life.

If your area of service does not correspond with your spiritual gift, you may become discouraged and frustrated and never find out where you really belong. You won't understand yourself, the gifts, or other Christians around you. In turn you could eventually become a spiritual dropout or end up doing nothing for God. *The key is for Christians to learn about spiritual gifts in the early stages of their Christian life.* This will give them a better handle on God's will for their lives and give them more direction as they start their Christian walk.

Whims will seldom stand the test of time. Yet, God-given desires will grow with time.

49

NEXT STEPS

Remember, one of the characteristics of a spiritual gift is *a supernatural desire or passion*. If God's will for your life is "whatever you desire" and your spiritual gift is a supernatural desire, then your spiritual gift is going to greatly influence what God's will is for your life.

In essence, God's will is not some superficial mythological truth that we cannot really grasp. God's will is part of the Christian's very being, and that being is strongly influenced by our God-given spiritual gifts.

In light of these facts, your emphasis should shift from trying to find God's will, to walking with God in the Spirit-filled life and finding and implementing your spiritual gifts. When this is done, God's will comes naturally.

FOR PERSONAL REFLECTION

1. Name the seven things that are God's will for your life.

2. What is the potential danger of the teaching above regarding your desires and God's will?

3. What is the relationship between God's will and spiritual gifts?

4. In what areas have you had a problem in the six steps of the Spirit-filled life as outlined in this chapter? How can the problem be overcome?

5. Where have you had a problem finding God's will for your life? What teaching in this chapter about God's will has helped you see His will better, and how?

6. How can you test your desires?

FOR GROUP DISCUSSION

THE WILL OF GOD IS NOT ...

1. _____

2. _____

3. _____

4 _____

5. _____

6. _____

THE WILL OF GOD IS...

God's will for your life is that you be:

1. _____ (2 Peter 3:9).

2. _____ (1 Thessalonians 4:3).

3. _____ (Ephesians 5:17-18).

4. _____ (1 Peter 2:13-15).

5. _____ (1 Peter 4:19; 33:17).

6. _____ (Romans 12:1-3).

"God will never reveal to you His unrevealed will if you are not willing to do His revealed will."

7. _____ (Psalm 37:4).

Understanding the will of God for your life is much easier when you know your spiritual gift(s).

Note: Answers for each chapter's "For Group Discussion" questions can be found on pages 183-184

GOD GIVES EVERY BELIEVER
AT LEAST ONE SPIRITUAL GIFT
AT THE TIME OF THE NEW BIRTH.
YET MANY CHRISTIANS LIVE MUCH
OR ALL OF THEIR CHRISTIAN LIFE
WITHOUT REALIZING THAT FACT OR
THE IMPACT OF SUCH A TRUTH.

4

SPIRITUAL GIFTS AND THEIR RELATIONSHIP TO THE BELIEVER

he Gospel Herald once published a story about a man who had climbed to the top of his field and was relatively well known in his country. It had been a long struggle and he had suffered many hardships and much ridicule as he climbed his way up the ladder of success. One day he sat contemplating his past and how he had made it to the top. He thought of all the influences and the people who had impacted his life. He thought of his deceased parents and all their years of labor and love. He thought too of his wife and her patience and sacrifice. His children were now grown, and they had made such an impact on his life and maturity through the years.

Finally, his thoughts wandered to the one event and one person who had influenced him to success more than all of these people and all the other events put together. He did not know the name of the man and the words only made up one sentence, but they had such an impact on his thinking that he was never the same again.

One summer afternoon, at a lake where he often swam with his friends, he was swimming alone. For some unknown reason, he suffered some physical problem and could swim no farther. He struggled for his life and was about to go under for the last time when he felt a man's strong arm lifting him from the water and taking him ashore. The boy never actually saw his rescuer's face and he could not recognize the voice. After making sure everything was well, the man left. As he did, the boy said, "Thank you, sir, for saving my life." The man replied, "You're welcome, son. See to it that you are worth saving."

It is similar with God, but even better: He values and loves us so much that He sent His only Son to save us. And even more, God gave us tools for sharing this wonderful news with others—spiritual gifts to do His work and the power of the Holy Spirit for using those gifts.

"I could never get in front of a group of people and speak or go door to door, talking to people about their soul," is the cry of many Christians. "Why, God hasn't given me any spiritual gifts. Maybe I'm just not spiritual enough for Him to trust me with any," they exclaim. If that were true, you would have no worth to God. But He must receive glory from our lives. In His providence He has provided a way for us to be "worth saving."

WHO HAS SPIRITUAL GIFTS?

Every true Christian has spiritual gifts. But as we shall see, God gives *every believer* at least one spiritual gift at the time of the New Birth. Yet many Christians live much or all of their Christian life without realizing that fact or the impact of such a truth.

The fact that every Christian receives at least one spiritual gift is evident in Scripture. All italics emphases are mine: "For by the grace given me I say to every one of you: Do not think of yourself more highly than you ought, but rather think of yourself with sober judgment, in accordance with the faith God has distributed to *each of you*" (Romans 12:3). "But *each of you* has your own gift from God; one has this gift, another has that" (1 Corinthians 7:7). "Now to *each one* the manifestation of the Spirit is given for the common good" (1 Corinthians 12:7). ". . . and he distributes them to *each one*, just as he determines" (1 Corinthians 12:11). "But to *each one* of us grace has been given as Christ apportioned it" (Ephesians 4:7). "*Each of you* should use whatever gift you have received to serve others, as faithful stewards of God's grace in its various forms" (1 Peter 4:10).

Clearly, from the context of these passages, God is talking about the Christian when He says "each one" or "each of you." In 1 Corinthians 12:29, Paul asks, "Are all apostles? Are all prophets? Are all teachers? Do all work miracles?" The obvious answer to Paul's series of questions is, "No." Therefore, we must conclude that all Christians have at least one spiritual gift and no Christian has them all.

Scripture indicates that you receive this gift at the very moment of your salvation conversion, along with the Holy Spirit, the Enabler Who empowers you to use those gifts effectively. William McRae writes, "They (the gifts) are given to every individual believer. This seems to demand that it be at conversion. If it were subsequent to salvation, some may have a gift and others may not have a gift. Paul and Peter indicate that everyone to whom they are writing has a gift, not that some have one and that others will receive one."

Humility is not a matter of denying one's God-given ability and potential, but of recognizing its presence, developing it and being thankful for it.

"What about 2 Timothy 1:6 and 1 Timothy 4:14?" They seem to indicate that one receives a spiritual gift by the laying on of hands. This seems to be a special case because Timothy was to be an apostolic delegate with great authority. That his authority came through the Apostle Paul is witnessed by the laying on of Paul's hands (see 2 Timothy 1:6).

Again McRae writes, "In 1 Timothy 4:14 it was 'with the laying on of the hands by the presbytery.' Paul's laying his hands on Timothy to bestow that gift on him followed the prophecy to Paul that Timothy should have a certain gift. This gift was then recognized by the elders who were associated with Paul in this matter."[1]

Some Christians, in an attempt to humble themselves, deny that God would give them a gift. To that statement comes the reply: Humility is the correct evaluation of your abilities and disabilities and living in the light of that evaluation. Humility is not a matter of denying one's God-given ability and potential, but of recognizing its presence, developing it and being thankful for it.

WOMEN AND SPIRITUAL GIFTS

Every gift and principle that pertains to men also pertains to women. In fact, in this age of emphasis upon the woman's place in society and, in particular, Christianity, it would be well to notice that there are two extremes in position concerning a woman's place in the ministry of God. The one extreme is to say the only place a woman can serve the Lord is to work in the nursery or the

55

kitchen at a church fellowship meeting. The other extreme is to say a woman could serve as senior pastor. Both ignore the biblical instruction for a woman to use her spiritual gift. The Bible is explicit in reference to some principles relating to women's leadership in the church. That teaching leaves room for women to exercise their spiritual gifts without violating God's directives. When God gave Christian women spiritual gifts, He gave them places in the church to use those gifts.

SPIRITUAL GIFTS DECLARE
THE PRESENCE OF THE HOLY SPIRIT

The Scriptures quoted earlier emphasize that Christians are to use their gifts to minister to others and that the power to use those gifts comes from the Holy Spirit. In fact, 1 Corinthians 12:7 seems to indicate that spiritual gifts are one of the manifestations, or indicators, of the Holy Spirit's presence in the life of the believer. Galatians 5:22-23 tells us about the fruit of the Spirit, which are behavior patterns that result from the presence of the Holy Spirit in the believer. On the other hand, the references that tell about spiritual gifts are referring to capacities given for service for Christ in the life of the believer. The "fruit of the Spirit" deals with attitude; gifts of the Spirit deal with action in service. Both are indications that the Holy Spirit is present in a person's life.

Spiritual gifts should not be confused with the fruit of the Holy Spirit. Christian leadership expert Bobby Clinton offers the following comparison in his book *Spiritual Gifts*:

GIFTS OF THE SPIRIT	FRUIT OF THE SPIRIT
Related primarily to the collective body of believers	*Related primarily to the individual believers in the body*
Related to ministry	*Related to character*
May be classified as to order of importance	*All are essential*
May be exercised in such a manner as to offend others and cause discord and division to the body	*Can never be misused*
No single believer receives all the gifts	*Every believer may bear all the fruits all the time*
No gift can be demanded of all believers	*All of us can be commanded to manifest the fruits*

The scriptural ideal seems to be the exercise of the gifts of the Spirit at the same time. Clinton goes on to indicate that spiritual gifts and the fruit of the Spirit are confirmation of the presence of the Holy Spirit in a life. Maturity is primarily indicated by Christ-likeness as seen in the fruit of the Spirit and may not include the presence of the gifts or the exercise of the gifts.[2] Fruit is an extension of the character of Christ; gifts are an extension of the ministry of Christ.[3] "The fruit of the Spirit is love, joy, peace, forbearance, kindness, goodness, faithfulness, gentleness and self-control" (Gal. 5:22).

> *Fruit is an extension of the character of Christ; gifts are an extension of the ministry of Christ.*

Spiritual gifts are not rewards. Gifts are given without regard to any degree of commitment. They are given by God's grace, not our faithfulness. They have nothing to do with how spiritual a person is. In 1 Corinthians 1:7, Paul says to the Corinthians, "you do not lack any spiritual gift." Yet, we know the Corinthians were very unspiritual and immature.

Spiritual gifts are not natural talent. You are given natural talents at your natural birth and spiritual talents (spiritual gifts) at your spiritual birth. Your responsibility as a Christian is to use both in service to glorify God.

Talents are available to the lost. Talents operate on a physical and social level. Talents alone cannot do God's work. God did not choose talents as the primary channel through which the Holy Spirit is to work.

Spiritual gifts are not places of service. Think *Shepherd* and you automatically think of the person behind the pulpit. Think *Evangelist* and you think of the traveling preacher. These are not always true descriptions, although most of the time people with these gifts do hold these positions. The problem comes with our modern-day terminology—this will be made clearer as we study the individual gifts.

Spiritual gifts are not age-specific ministries. Charles Ryrie writes, "There is no gift of young people's work or children's work. If there were, then there would be a gift of old people's work—a gift that the author has never heard anyone claim to have. Children, young and old adults all need the benefit from the exercise of gifts of pastor, teacher, etc."[4]

57

Spiritual gifts are not subject-specific ministries. Again, Ryrie writes, "There is no gift of writing or Christian education named in the Scripture. The gift of Teaching which is named, for instance, may be exercised through the education program of the church."[5] Music and athletics can also be put into this category. Teaching, Exhortation, and Mercy-Showing can be exercised through the talents of music and athletics.

Do not confuse spiritual gifts with the Christian's role or responsibly. For example, all Christians have been given the responsibility to tithe and reach out to others with the Gospel. Yet God has given a gift of Giving which allows some to give far beyond their tithe. Plus, the gift of Evangelism allows some to influence far more people with the Gospel than those without the gift. The danger comes when Christians use the lack of these gifts to neglect the responsibility to tithe or evangelize.

HOW MANY GIFTS ARE THERE?

In a recent survey I asked the question, "What is your spiritual gift?" Of the 72 adults responding, only 15 answered with what could be considered a valid name for a spiritual gift. Twenty-two gave no answer at all. Most amazing of all were the 28 who listed their gift by a term the Bible did not list. Many listed fruit of the Spirit (which is given to all Christians). The New Testament lists 21 gifts. However, most Bible scholars agree on a list of only 18. The definitions and characteristics of some gifts are so similar, some believe the Scriptures use synonyms in some cases. The following lists the gifts and Scripture references and suggests a simplified classification. It also shows which gifts are combined for our study.

CLASSIFICATION OF SPIRITUAL GIFTS

1. Miraculous Gifts

Apostle	1 Corinthians 12:28; Ephesians 4:11
Tongues	1 Corinthians 12:10, 28, 30
Interpretation	1 Corinthians 12:10, 30
Miracles	1 Corinthians 12:10, 28
Healing	1 Corinthians 12:9, 28

2. Enabling Gifts

Faith	1 Corinthians 12:9
Discernment	1 Corinthians 12:10
Wisdom	1 Corinthians 12:8
Knowledge	1 Corinthians 12:8

3. TEAM Gifts

Evangelism	Ephesians 4:11
Prophecy	Romans 12:6; Ephesians 4:11, 1 Corinthians 12:10, 28
Teaching	Romans 12:7; 1 Corinthians 12:28
Exhortation	Romans 12:8
Shepherding	Ephesians 4:11
Mercy-showing	Romans 12:8
Serving	Romans 12:7; 1 Corinthians 12:28
Giving	Romans 12:8
Administration	Romans 12:8; 1 Corinthians 12:28

59

THE MIRACULOUS GIFTS

The **miraculous gifts** are generally known today as *charismatic* or *sign gifts*. The term *charismatic* has become a generic term and probably takes in a broader base of denominations and groups than would voluntarily add themselves to the terminology. However, there are five basic positions (although each has many variations) on the miraculous, or charismatic, gifts.

1. ***Extreme Charismatic*** – This position contends that gifts are given through a second work of the Holy Spirit and that speaking in tongues is the evidence of the indwelling of the Holy Spirit. This view is rejected by most of Christianity. Those who hold this position speak in tongues, although most that speak in tongues do not hold this position. Those in this position usually hold the view that one *must* speak in tongues in order to be saved, thus adding to the Scriptures and thereby qualifying as a cult.

2. *Charismatic* – This position contends that all gifts are valid today and are given just as they were in the Early Church. They say that in order to experience the fullness of the Holy Spirit, all these gifts should be exercised in every local church. They reject the idea that tongues or any gift is *the* evidence of the fullness of the Holy Spirit. Most holding this position would profess having had some kind of charismatic experience at one time or another.

3. *Limited Charismatic* – This position says all gifts are valid today and given just as they were in the Early Church. However, God distributes these gifts within the "universal church," and different gifts manifest themselves in different local churches. Most of those who hold this position have never had a charismatic experience but are convinced that charismatic doctrine is valid. This is the middle-of-the-road position taken by most publishers and many mainline denominations.

4. *Non-Charismatic* – This position says all gifts are *not* valid today; therefore, the miraculous gifts should not be exercised in any church. It is their position that these gifts were given to the Early Church to establish or validate the authority of those who had the gift, and they were phased out by the end of the first century with the completion of the Canon of Scriptures (the Bible). They do not deny God heals. They deny that God gives any gift that allows man to heal.

5. *Anti-Charismatic* – This position takes about the same doctrinal stand as the non-charismatic position. They have a tendency, however, to take the abuses of the Extreme Charismatic and tag all charismatics with them. Their doctrinal disagreement usually leads to personal attacks. They usually tag all who hold to any of the charismatic positions as false teachers.

The purpose of this material is not to argue the pros and cons of the Charismatic Movement, nor is it to establish a doctrine concerning the charismatic gifts.

I wish to avoid the problem with much of the contemporary teaching on spiritual gifts. Many charismatics teach on the miraculous gifts with little or no emphasis on the remaining gifts while non-charismatics preach against the miraculous gifts, and in turn, put little or no emphasis on the remaining gifts. Or, as one pastor stated, "So much of what is written is either in defense of the charismatic position or an attack against it."

> *The enabling gifts are catalyst gifts that tie your spiritual qualities to your spiritual gifts.*

Developing the correct doctrinal position concerning the miraculous gifts is a must. Much good material is available to help you form a biblical doctrinal position. Be careful in your selections. So much is written on this subject, that regardless of any combination of thoughts you might come up with, you can find someone to agree with you. Without a doubt, the best book ever written on the subject is the Bible. It is much clearer that you might think. Read 1 Corinthians 12, 13 and 14 first, and ask God to direct you.

61

THE ENABLING GIFTS

The enabling gifts are catalyst gifts that tie your spiritual qualities to your spiritual gifts. A catalyst is an agent which, when added, speeds up the process of the other agents. In other words, the enabling gifts speed up the process of using the TEAM Gifts, thereby making them more effective. The enabling gifts are available to all Christians and should be sought by all.

The remaining gifts are the task-oriented gifts or what I call the TEAM Gifts. Most leaders, regardless of their position, would agree that these are also the church-growth-oriented gifts, the gifts that build the physical body. Therefore, I have limited the thrust of this study to these TEAM Gifts.

THE TEAM GIFTS

The third category of spiritual gifts is TEAM Gifts. They are job-, activity- ministry- or *task-oriented* gifts. They are functional. The TEAM Gifts are divided into two prominent types, *speaking* and *ministering* gifts. This does not mean you do not minister with the speaking gifts nor speak in the ministering gifts. In 1 Peter 4:9-11, Peter speaks of two groups in which to place the gifts. He says in verse 11, "If anyone speaks, they should do so as one who speaks the very words of God. If anyone serves, they should do so with the strength God provides."

Therefore, Peter gives us two groups of TEAM Gifts:

1. "Speaking" (the Greek word *laleo)* means to talk, utter words. Those who have the speaking gifts are Evangelists, Prophets, Teachers, Exhorters, and Shepherds.

2. "Ministering" gifts are support gifts. Ministers are not kings but "king-makers." These people are happy to work behind the scenes supporting the ones who have the speaking gifts. Ministering gifts include Shepherds, Mercy-Showers, Servers, Givers, and Administrators. Note that the Shepherd is on both lists. This is because of the many responsibilities God has given His "under-shepherds."

A detailed description with characteristics, strengths, weaknesses, and some areas where people with the TEAM Gifts are often misunderstood is covered in Chapter 5. A charted outline for each gift is given so that you can readily see the distinct characteristics of each gift. As you study them you need to understand they are generalized and there are as many variations and degrees as there are people who have these gifts.

NEXT STEPS

Anyone familiar with Scripture knows there are spiritual gifts. I want to reaffirm that God has given *everyone* in His family at least one spiritual gift and *everyone* in His family has a responsibility to use their gifts. It is important that the common misconceptions mentioned in this chapter be cleared up so that a *proper biblical foundation* is established so that everybody knows where the spiritual gifts come from. In other words, all of God's children need to know they are gifted and why they are gifted.

FOR PERSONAL REFLECTION

1. Which Christians have spiritual gifts, and when did they receive them?

2. Compare the "gifts of the Spirit" and the "fruit of the Spirit."

3. What part does each member of the Trinity play in spiritual gifts?

4. What are some things that you thought were spiritual gifts before studying this chapter, which are not listed in the Scriptures? How does a proper perspective in these areas affect your thinking about the ministry of the church?

5. Why is it important for churches to recognize the spiritual gifts of women and to help them develop their gifts?

6. What part does humility play in the development and use of your spiritual gifts?

FOR GROUP DISCUSSION

Who has spiritual gifts?

1. Every true_____

   has at least_____

   1 Corinthians 7:7, 12:7, Ephesians 4:7, 1 Peter 4:10

   No one has_____

   1 Corinthians 12:29

2. Every Christian _____

3. God _____which spiritual gift you receive.

   1 Corinthians 12:11, 12:18

Do not confuse spiritual gifts with:

1. The _____of the Spirit.

GIFTS OF THE SPIRIT	FRUIT OF THE SPIRIT
Relate primarily to the collective body of believers.	*Relate primarily to the individual believer.*
Relate to ministry.	*Relate to character.*
May be classified as to order of importance.	*All are essential.*
May be misused to cause discord.	*Can never be misused.*
No single believer receives all the gifts.	*Every believer may bear all the fruits all the time.*
No gift can be demanded of all believers.	*All of us can be commanded to manifest the fruits.*

63

2. Natural_____

3. A _____ of service.

4. An _____ ministry.

5. A _____ ministry.

6. Christian _____.

Gift Classifications

Most scholars agree on _____ classifications of gifts.

1. _____ gifts.

Positions on Miraculous Gifts

a. _____

b. _____

c. _____

d. _____

e. _____

Two Other Types of Gifts Groups Are ...

2. _____ gifts.

3. _____ gifts.

Note: Answers for each chapter's "For Group Discussion" questions can be found on pages 183-184

5

TEAM MINISTRY

People will support the church that meets the needs in their lives or touches the needs and lives of their loved ones. Not only must the church meet the needs, but it must also meet the needs when they occur. The church that can meet a person's specific need when it occurs will have the best chance of reaching that person for Christ.

There are two kinds of needs: felt needs and real needs. Sometimes the felt needs are not real needs, or the real needs are not felt by a person. The church must meet those needs, sometimes pointing out the real need in the person's life so that it becomes a felt need. Other times the felt need must be met first in order to discover the real need. Therefore, the church must meet both felt and real needs.

How can that best be done? By using the TEAM Gifts in the lives of the members to reach the needs of non-believers in the community. For every need in the life of an unsaved person, there is a gift that helps reach that person for Christ. When the lost receive Christ, there are still needs to meet. The TEAM can come to the rescue, meeting those needs through the spiritual gifts God gave for that purpose.

What I really want to explain here is how the balanced church meets all the needs that exist in the body. But first I must address the *purpose* of the church. For only a church that is effectively fulfilling its God-given purpose can effectively minister to the needs of its community and members.

When people talk of TEAM building in the church, much of the emphasis is put on "ministry teams." This is good, but there is another larger "ministry TEAM" in the church with even greater potential—the local church itself. (A local church is a single congregation, made up of many members. The Body of Christ [some use the term "Universal Church"] is made up of many local churches. The references here are to the single congregation—the local church.)

A healthy church meets the needs of its members and reaches out to the community it serves. A healthy church is balanced as Paul spells out in Ephesians 4:16, "From him the whole body, joined and held together by every supporting ligament, grows and builds itself up in love, as each part does its work." A healthy church *grows* (increases in numbers by reaching people for Christ) and edifies or *builds itself up* (ministers to the needs within its own body). A healthy church ministers outside the body and to the body from within the body. A healthy church balances its ministry with the gifts God has given it.

The "TEAM Ministry" chart that follows explains how God has given us spiritual gifts to balance the church and to meet needs. Let me give you a little background as to how this chart was developed.

A number of years ago, I started teaching an adult Sunday school class. I was young and had never taught before, nor had I received any teacher training. I realized that if I were going to be successful, not only did I need to teach certain material, I had to meet definite needs in the lives of my students. My classes didn't always go the way I had hoped. Whenever I bombed out, being an analytical person, I always asked the question, "Why didn't it work?" I really wanted to do it right, so I would head to the Christian bookstore to buy a new book.

My studies reinforced the fact that if I was going to minister and reach people, I had to meet several needs in their lives—not just one or two needs—to effectively minister to the *whole* person. In fact, I came up with a list of eleven needs that you'll see in the "Team Ministry" chart.

Later, through an in-depth study of spiritual gifts, I was amazed as God pointed out to me the correlation between these needs and the spiritual gifts. The characteristics of each gift met a need that was evident. The more I studied, the more I could see how they dovetailed together perfectly. On one side were the people's needs that had to be met, and on the other side were the gifts with dominant characteristics that would minister to the needs.

The chart titled "Team Ministry" is the result of that study. The left side lists the needs that the church must meet in a person's life if the person is to mature as a Christian. The other side of the chart is the gift that predominantly ministers to that particular need.

MAN'S NEEDS

1. SALVATION
3. AWARENESS OF SIN
5. DOCTRINE
7. TO KNOW HOW
9. SHEPHERDING
11. COMFORTING
13. A HELPING HAND
15. FINANCIAL AID
17. LEADERSHIP
19. FELLOWSHIP
22. A MATURE CHRISTIAN

GOD'S PROVISIONS

2. EVANGELISTS
4. PROPHETS
6. TEACHERS
8. EXHORTERS
10. SHEPHERDS
12. MERCY-SHOWERS
14. SERVERS
16. GIVERS
18. ADMINISTRATORS
20. ENTIRE BODY
23. THE "TEAM"

21. TO SERVE THEIR FELLOW MAN

24. LASTING GROWTH

If I was going to minister and reach people, I had to meet several needs in their lives—not just one or two needs—to effectively minister to the whole person.

Let's look at the needs one at a time and see how God has equipped the church to minister to them. (The numbering system will help you follow the chart. Please note that when the term "man" is used, it means "humankind" which includes male and female.)

1. NEED: Salvation – Romans 3:23 says, "For all have sinned, and come short of the glory of God." Which TEAM member meets this need in a person's life?

2. PROVISION: Evangelist – This does not mean the Evangelist is the only person in a church to lead people to a saving knowledge of Jesus Christ. But, if you took a poll, you would see that the Evangelist is the person who probably reaches eighty or ninety percent of those who come to Christ. Evangelists are "salespeople" for Christ. They are aggressive and confrontational.

Confrontational or presentational Evangelists (called soul-winners by some) are the type of people who always try to motivate others to reach out to lost people. They give the testimonies like, "I went on a plane trip and I sat next to a guy who wasn't saved." They end the story by saying, "As the plane touched down, the gentleman beside me bowed his head and accepted Christ as his Savior." They get on an elevator with a "sinner" on the sixth floor and get off on the twelfth floor with a "saint."

Again, I need to stress that gifted Evangelists are not the only ones who can lead people to Christ. The fact is that Evangelists lead more people to the point of decision even though someone else may have influenced the people and laid the groundwork for their decision to accept Christ as Savior. All Christians have the role to witness through using their own lives and God-given gifts; however, some are given a special gift for Evangelism. The importance of understanding the role or responsibility of the Evangelist versus the responsibility of all Christians to witness is so great that all of

68

Chapter 6 is dedicated to this subject.

3. *NEED: Awareness of sin* – Someone once said that the world is so churchy and the church is so worldly that we can't tell the difference. The truth is the world has so much influence on us even as Christians that we sometimes have a hard time recognizing sin. Unfortunately, we have become somewhat desensitized and participate in things that only a few years ago we would have clearly recognized as sin.

4. *PROVISION: Prophet* – God has provided a special gift in the church to make people aware of their sins. Here we are speaking of the New Testament gift of Prophecy, which is forthtelling, not the Old Testament position of the foretelling prophet. Prophets tell God's Word like it is. They usually have the ability to see what's wrong in people's lives and churches and point it out. Their weakness is they are so focused on what is wrong; they fail to see what is right. Their ministry often manifests itself through preaching and public speaking, where they usually point out sin and what is wrong. They get excited, step on toes, and preach for conviction. They want to help you see the sin in your life so you can change it, and the wrong in society so you can make a difference. Their preaching and speaking will stir your heart and sometimes make you mad. Hellfire and brimstone-type preachers have the gift of Prophecy to make people aware of their sin and to encourage repentance. They are conduits for revival and change.

Someone once said that the world is so churchy and the church is so worldly that we can't tell the difference.

5. *NEED: Knowing what is right* – Not only do we have a crying need to know how to live right, but also to learn the principles for right living—*what is right*. Only God's Word can truly tell us what is right.

6. *PROVISION: Teacher* – The person who meets the Church's need in helping people discern right from wrong is the Teacher. *Didasko* is the Greek word meaning "to teach": to communicate knowledge, to relay facts or to make known. Teachers are always studying and communicating the norms, standards, and doctrines of Scripture to others, verbally and through the written word. Teachers are willing to dig deep to find the "true" meaning of Scripture and make all the pieces fit. They are detail-oriented and put great emphasis on word usage and pronunciation. Teachers tend to be very content-oriented, yet can be weak on application. They mostly teach chronologically. Those who are high in the gift of Teaching and low in the other teaching or speaking gifts may not make the best Sunday school teachers. I'll explain in a minute.

7. NEED: To know "how." Many times we are convicted that we need to make changes in our lives but the problem is we just don't know how. We need practical steps in order to go forward.

8. PROVISION: Exhorter – The one who provides such practical "how-to" steps in a person's life is the *Exhorter*. Exhorters spend their time teaching people how to do things; they are application-oriented people. Exhorters have practical steps for everything. Unlike the Teacher that teaches chronologically, the Exhorter teaches topically; pulling Scriptures from throughout the Bible to support a single topic. They also motivate, encourage, and excite people, leading them to get more done. They make great counselors because they tend to provide practical solutions to problems.

9. NEED: To be cared for. It has been said that when a sheep lies down with its head facing downhill it can't get up by itself; it needs the shepherd to help it. Who meets that need in a person's life? The Shepherd . . .

10. PROVISION: The Shepherd – Shepherds have a caretaker approach to leadership. They are burdened to teach God's Word and to care for the people around them. They protect and shelter their sheep. This gift is not limited to the position of senior pastor. Many Christians have the gift of Shepherding, especially women. It can be used in a variety of positions inside and outside the church from Sunday school teachers to Scout den leaders. People with the gift of Shepherd make the best Sunday school and small group leaders because their desire is to teach and *shepherd* the group while those with the dominant gift of Teaching tend to give content only.

11. NEED: To be comforted. Who would meet that need? The Mercy-Shower . . .

12. PROVISION: The Mercy-Shower – Those with this gift are usually soft-spoken but outgoing people who always seem to know what to say—or what not to say—when someone hurts. They empathize with people, *feeling* their hurts and joys, rather than just having sympathy for them. If a tragedy were to happen in your life, you would appreciate a visit or call from the person with the gift of Mercy-Showing because he or she would help you better deal with the pain. Mercy-Showers provide a special support that others don't. They attract people who are hurting, because they have the ability to put themselves in someone else's shoes. They also attract people who are experiencing times of joy. People like to share their happy days with them as well, because Mercy-Showers rejoice with them. Mercy-Showers provide emotional support and encouragement no matter what the situation. Mercy-Showers are good listeners.

13. NEED: A helping hand. In order to keep a church building from falling down, people who are willing to do the maintenance and take care of the building are needed.

14. PROVISION: The Server – The Server is very content doing the physical labor around the church and many times at your house. Servers get fulfillment out of doing what many people see as menial

71

tasks. They do not need or like the spotlight on them and are content working behind the scenes. They are not kings but kingmakers. God has given the gift of Serving to many people in all churches.

Let me stop here and address a misconception about the gift of Serving. Occasionally I'll bump into someone who has the "I can'ts." They say something like, "I can't sing, I can't preach, I can't teach, I can't lead; I must 'just' have the gift of Serving." This belittles the gift of Service. It implies that God gives the gift of Serving to those who can't do anything else. This is simply not true.

I heard a story once about a man who walked into the office of the Raiders pro football team when they were located in L.A. No one was at the receptionist desk, but a woman was at the copy machine. Turning to her he questioned, "Young lady, what is your job here?" expecting her to say, "I'm the receptionist." Her answer, "My job is to win the Super Bowl." She recognized herself as an important part of the TEAM even though she would never score a touchdown.

She knew that even though the spotlight and the TV cameras would never pursue her, she helped her TEAM win. The same is true if you have the gift of Serving, or as far as that goes, any gift. You are a vital part of the TEAM and your TEAM is incomplete without you. You may never be in the spotlight either, but you'll have the satisfaction knowing you are where God wants you and you are needed to help your TEAM win: to fulfill the Great Commission. First Corinthians 12:22 says, "On the contrary, those parts of the body that seem to be weaker are indispensable." Note that Paul did not say that some members *are weaker,* but by adding the word *seem,* he recognizes that we often think some members have less value than others, when this isn't true.

15. **NEED: Financial aid.** The ministries and the missions of the church need financial support. Plus, from time to time people in our community need assistance. Enter the Giver . . .

16. *PROVISION: The Giver* – The person who meets this tangible and often financial need is the Giver. Givers are very missions minded. It's not unusual to see a church with several Givers in it supporting many missions projects. While all Christians have the responsibility to tithe, God has given some the ability to give far beyond their normal tithe. Giving starts where tithing ends. Many people with the gift of Giving have the ability to make lots of money, but not always.

They usually like to keep their giving private and don't seek recognition. Helping their fellow man in need and supporting special projects and ministries of the church blesses them. They are good stewards and want to know that their money is being put to good use. I'm thankful that as I went back to graduate school people who had the gift of Giving helped my family and me with financial needs. We probably never would have been able to make it without their help.

At this point, I need to stress that giving and serving are two gifts on which the church really needs to place an extra emphasis today, because we've allowed government to take over in these areas. Christians will give to churches to add a wing on the church, but when it comes to giving to an individual, people hesitate and either give once or only give a small amount, if anything at all. We have allowed government to make up for the Christian's failure to do what is right.

When a person in the church has problems, Christians usually try to "help" by pointing the person in another direction. "Can't you borrow the money to get straightened out?" "Surely there is some type of welfare program that will help." In some circumstances the response is, "You can have the money if you sign a note and pay it back monthly with interest." We're telling people to go somewhere else, but God says that the church should meet those needs in people's lives through Christians in TEAM Ministry. Romans 12:13 says, "Distributing to the necessity of saints; given to hospitality" (KJV)—and the saints are the Christians "given to hospitality."

73

It's our job to take care of and to meet the needs of those people in the body, and not pawn them off on government agencies. It was never the government's job to start with (read Acts Chapter 6). Government picked up on it simply because Christians were failing by not ministering with the gifts that God had given them. The gifts of Giving and Serving are the predominant gifts that can help with these physical needs. I also believe that these two gifts are the most prevalent ones in most of our churches. However, people with continual financial problems don't need financial assistance, they need financial counseling.

17. NEED: Leadership. The fact is, most people are followers. In order to reach a goal, eighty-four percent of people need a totally planned, supervised program. If the program is carefully laid out, fourteen percent of people have the ability to meet that goal with little supervision. Only two percent of people have the ability to create a dream and carry it through to completion by themselves.

74

18. PROVISION: The Administrator – They are the leaders. When you think of the Administrator, don't think of some kind of a glorified file clerk. Leading, ruling, organizing, governing, and administering are words that come from the same Greek word in different translations of the Scriptures. The Greek word *Kubernesis* was a steersman for a ship. He had the responsibility of bringing a ship into the harbor—past the rocks and shoals under all types of pressures. Administrators are "take charge" people who jump in and start giving direction when no one else is doing so (or sometimes when someone else is in charge). They put a plan on paper and start delegating responsibility. The committee or group reports back to them and they work the whole scheme of the program together.

Anywhere people are willing to wrap up their lives in the lives of other people, you'll see happier, more contented, and less troubled people—simply because they are meeting a God-given need.

19. *NEED: Fellowship.* Who meets this need? The fellowship of believers.

20. *PROVISION: The entire body.* All the Administrators, Servers, Givers, Exhorters, Prophets, Teachers, Evangelists, Mercy-Showers and Shepherds meet the need for fellowship. All these people combined together, the entire body, meet the fellowship need in a person's life. By the way, polls have shown that most people who start attending a church do so for the fellowship they enjoy. They go to a church where they have friends and can gain emotional support from other people.

21. *NEED and PROVISION: People serving other people.* Take another look at the TEAM MINISTRY chart on page 67, and running up the center of the graph is a vertical heading entitled "To Serve Their Fellow Man." I call this the "catalyst need" because it ties together the whole concept of spiritual gifts with the needs that must be met. The provision is built *into* the need (thus the heading NEED *and* PROVISION): *Man serving his fellow man.* This need is put into the hearts of all people—Christian and non-Christian alike—by God. It means people wrapping their lives up in the lives of others. Anywhere people are willing to wrap up their lives in the lives of other people, you'll see happier, more contented, and less troubled people—simply because they are meeting a God-given need. As Christians, we need to serve our fellow man by ministering through our spiritual gifts. A television commercial once promoted, "People helping people, that's what life is all about." That *is* what life is all about. The most miserable people I know are selfish, concerned only with themselves and their own welfare. They are miserable and they make everyone around them just as miserable as they are. Let's not be misery makers, but encouragers and helpers through exercising our God-given spiritual gifts in ministry to and with others.

75

22. NEED: Becoming a mature Christian. Let's add up the entire left side of the chart (as if this were a math problem). What is the sum or outcome when the body of Christ walks in all the gifts? The development of *mature Christians.* After you have met all these needs in a person's life, he or she becomes mature. For every need the church fails to meet, the individual will be that much less mature. But, the closer we come to meeting all the needs, the more mature the person will become.

Tragically though, many churches miss one, two, three, or even all of the top four needs. To keep from making this mistake, we need to understand the *biblical procedure* for training Christians. Second Timothy 3:16 states, "All Scripture is given by inspiration of God, and is profitable (for four things) for doctrine, for reproof, for correction, for instruction in righteousness" (KJV). We quote this Scripture very often to support the fact that we have an inerrant Bible. But, let's look one step further and see the *biblical procedure* for training Christians. The procedure is first, doctrine; second, reproof; third, correction; and fourth, instruction. I don't think it is any accident these four items appear in your Bible in this order.

Doctrine is the norms and standards of the Scriptures. It teaches the standards by which we must govern our lives and our ministries. Doctrine is not the process of teaching, but the product of teaching. The second step is *reproof.* To reprove, you show what is wrong. Next is *correction.* To correct, you show what is right. *Instruction* is simply "how to" or practical application. Notice the relationship. First, the dominant ministry of the *Prophet* is simply pointing out *what is wrong,* and the dominant ministry of the *Teacher* is simply pointing out *what is right.*

The dominant ministry of the *Exhorter* is simply telling *how to* do it. We have a tendency to ignore some of these people, most often the Prophet. The Prophet makes us uncomfortable. After all, who wants someone stepping on their toes pointing out what's wrong with their life? We usually try to keep those who make us uncomfortable out of our lives. Many churches lack a gifted Teacher and a sound doctrinal foundation for their ministry. The person who is doctrine oriented is usually fact oriented rather than practical-application oriented. But a good Teacher, teaching theology, doctrine and prophecy week in and week out, without giving practical application, will have a frustrated congregation.

One of the most evident things lacking in meeting people's needs is simple, practical, "how to" teaching.

One of the most evident things lacking in meeting people's needs is simple, practical, "how to" teaching. For instance, consider the man who says, "I know I am coming up short as a father, and I know I do things wrong, but I'm tired of people telling me what I'm doing wrong. I want somebody to show me *how to* become a better father." On the other hand, you can't teach a man how to be a better father if you haven't first convicted him that he needs to be a better father. Without conviction, practical teaching will go in one ear and out the other. At the same time, the practical Teacher cannot be effective if his or her teaching is not based on the sound doctrine—proper theology—that is brought to light by the gifted Teacher.

Sometimes Teachers can teach to lead to conviction and explain "how to." Besides Teaching, they have the secondary gift of Exhortation. However, most often the Prophet gets us stirred up or convicted, then the practical Exhorter comes in and gives us the "how to," based on the doctrinal teachings of the Teacher, thus enabling us to change our lives. This type of situation further emphasizes the balance and cooperation within the body as described in the Bible when it deals with spiritual gifts.

TEAM Ministry does not mean exclusiveness. Example: A man comes into your church for help and the secretary asks, "Do you know Christ?" He says, "No." So she says, "In that case, first, you

77

need to go to the end of the hall and see Rev. Evangelist, so he can lead you to Christ. Then you need to go across the hall to see Dr. Teacher so he can show you what's right. Then go upstairs and let Counselor Exhorter show you how to solve your problem." Team Ministry involves people who will excel in these different areas of the ministry because of their God-given gifts. There will always be some overlap in all the areas of giftedness and ministry.

23. PROVISION: The TEAM – When the right side of the chart is added together, it totals The Team. The **Team** (the local church) is a group of Christians indwelled and empowered by the Holy Spirit. No doubt about it, this is the most powerful force on this earth. For years we have let this force lie nearly dormant. We have the most powerful force on earth, yet by doing nothing with it, we're letting the world and humanism take over our schools, our government, our country, and our world. As said by 18th century philosopher Edmund Burke, "All it takes for evil to triumph is for good men to do nothing."

24. Need + Provision = Lasting Growth – When you add all these met needs and active gifts together, you get *Lasting Growth*. For lasting growth, the church has to meet *all* these needs in the members' lives. When you miss some of these needs, people are left incomplete. They subconsciously look to fulfill the missing needs. In many cases, they're not even aware the needs exist. All they know is there's emptiness in their lives, and they just move on. They look for another church that can meet their needs. Sometimes after moving through several churches, they drop out completely, thinking that no church can meet their needs. Of course, very few churches can minister perfectly to *all* these needs. But, the more needs are met, the more effective the church will be in achieving lasting growth.

BALANCE FOR HEALTH

Some churches are strong on outreach. They're leading people to accept Christ as Lord and Savior, but at the same time people are going out the back door. These churches lack a good support program to follow up the evangelism. Some churches have good teaching ministries, but don't evangelize. The biblical ideal is to achieve balance. The balanced church is a growing and healthy church.

THE ANALOGY OF THE BODY

In three places where Paul writes on spiritual gifts (Romans 12, 1 Corinthians 12 and Ephesians 4), he uses a five-way analogy: 1) the human body, 2) the body of Christ, 3) the church, 4) the members, and 5) the spiritual gifts of those members. The church with the various spiritual gifts is compared to the parts of the human body. First Corinthians 12:12-27 says:

Just as a body, though one, has many parts, but all its many parts form one body, so it is with Christ. For we were all baptized by one Spirit so as to form one body—whether Jews or Gentiles, slave or free—and we were all given the one Spirit to drink. Even so the body is not made up of one part but of many. Now if the foot should say, "Because I am not a hand, I do not belong to the body," it would not for that reason stop being part of the body. And if the ear should say, "Because I am not an eye, I do not belong to the body," it would not for that reason stop being part of the body. If the whole body were an eye, where would the sense of hearing be? If the whole body were an ear, where would the sense of smell be? But in fact God has placed the parts in the body, every one of them, just as he wanted them to be. If they were all one part, where would the body be? As it is, there are many parts, but one body. The eye cannot say to the hand, "I don't need you!" And the head cannot say to the feet, "I don't need you!" On the contrary, those parts of the body that seem to be weaker are indispensable, and the parts that we think are less honorable

79

> The TEAM (the local church) is a group of Christians indwelled and empowered by the Holy Spirit. No doubt about it, this is the most powerful force on this earth.

we treat with special honor. And the parts that are unpresentable are treated with special modesty, while our presentable parts need no special treatment. But God has put the body together, giving greater honor to the parts that lacked it, so that there should be no division in the body, but that its parts should have equal concern for each other. If one part suffers, every part suffers with it; if one part is honored, every part rejoices with it. Now you are the body of Christ, and each one of you is a part of it.

> The worst thing you could do by being a little toe is being a little toe that goes to sleep.

Paul's analogy of the human body is an excellent example of the function of spiritual gifts within the church TEAM. Take the human body and chop off a hand—as a matter of fact, remove arms, legs, ears, nose, eyes, teeth, and hair. And although the body is seriously handicapped, it does not cease to function; it just doesn't function efficiently.

The question is: *when does the body function most effectively and efficiently?* The answer is when every member is there and doing what it is he or she is supposed to do. When you write with your hands, walk on your feet, hear with your ears, see with your eyes, and all members are working together for one common goal, you are balanced.

To develop this effective TEAM, all the gifts must be operating in one local church, thus meeting the needs of all the people in that church or community. We complement each other and we meet each other's needs; therefore, we make an effective TEAM.

THE "LITTLE TOE" PRINCIPLE

You might say, "I know that I'm part of the body, but I'm just the little toe. I'm really not important. I don't have much part in the body, and I'm not effective at all."

I know a man who lost his little toe in an accident. He found out just how important that little toe is. You may not think the little toe is very important, but the little toe has much to do with the balance of the body. Likewise, if you're the little toe in your church, you have much to do with its balance.

The little toe really doesn't have any effective muscles in it. If you lean off balance, and start to fall, your little toe has no muscles to stop you from falling. But it immediately sends a signal to the brain that says, "out of balance." Then the brain sends a signal to various other muscles to contract to keep you from falling. My friend without a little toe really had to pay attention to what he was doing. If he ran, walked too fast, or if he was not paying attention, he'd lose his balance and fall. If you're the little toe in your church, you have the same effect on your church (the body of Christ) as this man's little toe had on his body.

The worst thing you could do by being a little toe is be a little toe that goes to sleep. The little toe that goes to sleep, just like the foot that goes to sleep, affects the whole body. You could be part of what's holding back your church. Whichever part you fulfill, your role is very important. You are important to an effectively functioning body.

NEXT STEPS

Everyone has needs. God has always used men and women to accomplish His plan. His plan is for everyone's needs to be met; therefore, His plan is for His people to meet the needs of others. Every person in the church should have a part in meeting the needs of people in the church and community.

81

The more individual church members minister in this manner, the more balanced the church will be. The more balanced the church is, the healthier it will be. The healthier the church is, the more it will grow numerically and spiritually. The more lasting numerical and spiritual growth takes place, the more God will be honored.

FOR PERSONAL REFLECTION

1. What is the two-fold purpose of the church?

2. Why is it important to meet people's needs in the church?

3. What is the end result of meeting all of humankind's needs as listed on the TEAM Ministry chart?

4. How have some gifted people met needs in your life? What were the needs and who met them?

5. In what ways can the "biblical procedure" for training Christians help solve problems and meet needs in your life?

6. In what ways have you been hampered when a part of your body did not function? What does that teach you about the church?

FOR GROUP DISCUSSION

Examine the Five-Way Analogy of Spiritual Gifts

Use the following Scriptures and refer to the appropriate text in the chapter—
1 Corinthians 12, Romans 12, and Ephesians 4

1. _____

2. _____

3. _____

4. _____

5. _____

Fill in the blank TEAM Ministry Chart on the following page with the corresponding needs and provisions, and discuss. How does the TEAM Ministry chart on the next page make sense to you, and in what ways is it confusing?

Note: Answers for each chapter's "For Group Discussion" questions can be found on pages 183-184

TEAM MINISTRY

MAN'S NEEDS

GOD'S PROVISIONS

1 ....

2 ....

3 ....

4 ....

5 ....

6 ....

7 ....

8 ....

9 ....

21

10 ....

11 ....

12 ....

13 ....

14 ....

15 ....

16 ....

17 ....

18 ....

19 ....

20 ....

22 ....

23 ....

24 ....

HAVE YOU EVER HEARD THE EXPRESSION, "YOU CAN'T GET A MAN SAVED UNTIL YOU GET HIM LOST"? WELL, YOU CANNOT GET A NON-SEEKER "SAVED" UNTIL YOU TURN HIM OR HER INTO A SEEKER. NON-SEEKERS LACK THE MENTAL ENVIRONMENT FOR ACCEPTING THE GOSPEL. THEREFORE, WE MUST CHANGE THE ENVIRONMENT IN WHICH THEY THINK. TO DO THIS WE MUST BUILD TRUSTING RELATIONSHIPS WITH THEM.

6

THE GIFT OF EVANGELISM AND ITS RELATIONSHIP TO EVANGELISM

Only two groups of people in every church are responsible for doing evangelism. Let me state that again: only two groups of people in every church are responsible for doing evangelism. Group one is Christians *with* the gift of Evangelism. Group two is Christians *without* the gift of Evangelism.

Why do I say it that way? Because we need to recognize that if there are two distinct groups of people who are responsible for doing evangelism, then we need two distinct methods to fit the two different groups of people. Literally scores of evangelism programs are available to the church today. Most evangelism programs, however, have been written by people with the gift of Evangelism, for people with the gift of Evangelism, and unfortunately imposed upon all. The solution to this problem lies in recognizing the role of spiritual gifts in evangelism.

To properly understand the relationship of spiritual gifts to evangelism, we must first understand the difference between the gift of Evangelism and the command to evangelize. Let's take a look at both.

THE REAL KEY TO REACHING PEOPLE FOR CHRIST

Years ago I owned a business next to a new car dealership. I became friends with the owner, Frank. One day he asked if I knew anyone looking for a job. He needed to hire another salesperson. I knew someone who needed a job but I didn't know how good a salesperson he would make. Frank hired my friend Jack, anyway. About six weeks later I walked into Frank's office. He was on the phone talking to a customer. While waiting I noticed a sales chart on the wall. It read something like this, "Frank 18; Bobby 21; Joe 13; Jack 36." To my surprise, it appeared that my friend Jack was a much better salesperson than I thought.

When Frank got off the phone I casually asked, "How's Jack doing?" To which Frank replied, "Not too bad." Astonished, I said, "Not too bad! He's already sold twice as many cars as you this month. How can you say, 'Not too bad'?" To which Frank replied, "Wait till next month." I asked, "Why? What's going to happen next month?" Frank answered, "Next month he runs out of *friends and relatives*."

At the risk of comparing evangelism to selling used cars I later came to the conclusion that *the key to reaching people for Christ is friends and family,* or "existing relationships." This conclusion is supported by a survey done in scores of seminars conducted by Church Growth Institute with thousands of participants. This exhaustive survey showed that the number one means that influenced people to accept Christ or start coming to church was a friend or relative.

What Influences People to Come to Church?

Ads/marketing — 2%

Organized Visitation — 6%

Pastoral Contact — 6%

Invitation from a Friend or Relative — 86%

Because of this, we need to evaluate evangelism methods in the light of reality as well as Scripture.

UNDERSTANDING EVANGELISM METHODS

Two basic positions on evangelism dominate Christianity. Although a variety of Scriptures are used for their support, both positions would view their interpretation of the Great Commission as their foundation (Matthew 28:18-20, Mark 16:15-18, Luke 24:47-48, John 20:21-23, and Acts 1:8).

Position #1 – Confrontational Evangelism: This position interprets these combined Scriptures as saying that every Christian has the responsibility to share Christ (witness) to every non-saved person.

Furthermore, witnessing goes beyond the personal testimony, requiring both the presentation of the Gospel and the pursuit of a decision.

Most people holding this position contend that the Great Commission was given to the individual, not the church, and that we all have a personal responsibility to fulfill it. When speaking of the Great Commission, they most often quote Mark 16:15 and emphasize "preach the Gospel to all creation" (or "every creature," as it says in the KJV). They believe that leading others to Christ is the most important work a person can do.

This position generally rejects the idea that God has given a gift that would enable certain Christians to become more effective or aggressive "soul winners" than others, therefore removing any and all excuses of the "non-gifted" for not soul winning. Many believe that evangelism in Ephesians 4 is a calling of God and an office of the church, and therefore given to those called into full-time evangelistic ministries (for example, D. L. Moody, Billy Sunday, John R. Rice, Luis Palau, etc.). Their belief, as they communicate it, is that God will enable any yielded person to overcome the obstacles that would hinder him or her from becoming the kind of soul winner they themselves are.

Within this first position are two extremes or variations. One extreme would say things like: "If you are not leading two or three people to Christ each week, maybe you should question your own salvation." Or, "The evidence of the fullness of the Holy Spirit is not whether you are speaking in tongues, but rather, how many people you are winning to Christ." (All Scripture supported, of course.)

The other would say: "The Scriptures don't say you have to get results; you only have to sow seeds." This leads to a simplified three-point tract that enables you to present the Gospel to a hundred homes on a Saturday afternoon without any need for follow-up.

87

Both extremes have messages entitled "Go" and use the passage in Acts saying "house to house," assuring us that this was the way they did it in the early church; therefore, it's the *only* successful way for us to evangelize today. Historically—and particularly before the digital age—both were heavy users of tracts but would insist that they should never be used as a "cop-out" to personal witnessing. Many times they left most Christians feeling unspiritual or inferior for not participating in the visitation program.

Though much of the focus of both camps today is based on reaching people online as well as in person, both of these extremes often border on "Easy Believe-ism" (decision-getting without true conversion) and "Guilt-trip Evangelism" (motivation by guilt).

Position #2 – Lifestyle Evangelism: This position is quite the opposite of the first. Their reaction to the heavy emphasis on soul winning gives the Great Commission a different twist. They stress the passage in Matthew and point out that the Commission really emphasizes teaching, which they do well. They would agree that the Great Commission conveys the idea that all should be witnesses—and a witness is "living your life so that others might see Christ in you." You may hear one say, "Our job is to sow seeds, but not verbal seeds, for actions speak louder than words."

Many holding this position would say that the gift of Evangelism *is* an office of the church, therefore making it the duty of the paid staff to do the evangelizing. Still others would say, "The gift of Evangelism is available to all, but I don't have it," therefore relieving themselves of the responsibility of sharing the Gospel with others.

This group will accuse the first group of being over-zealous and offering an overly simplified plan for salvation, while they have a very complicated and theological explanation for God's redemption of humankind.

An extreme for this position slides into the hyper-Calvinism philosophy.

Lifestyle Evangelism is a philosophy based on an over-reaction to Confrontational Evangelism. Therefore, the problem with Lifestyle Evangelism is not its philosophy or methodology, but the attitude in which it was conceived. A person holding either of the two positions must evaluate his or her own attitude for holding that position.

EVALUATION OF BOTH POSITIONS

Both Confrontational and Lifestyle positions are built on their interpretation of the Great Commission. While both positions have good scriptural arguments, neither side would agree with such a statement about the other.

The most important thing to notice about both positions is they fit the gifts, personalities, motivations, temperaments, character strengths and weaknesses of each group.

We must recognize each position for what it is—a *method*, not a scriptural mandate; a method that basically fits the dominant gift of each group. Both groups border on becoming "theo-methodologists." Their method becomes their theology.

Both positions are effective. The attitude that insinuates *everyone* should fit into *their* position is wrong. Some people, either by gift or personality, can never become outgoing or confrontational. Others, because of their gift or personality, would never be able to give testimony only by their actions—they must be outgoing and verbal.

BALANCE IS THE ANSWER

A third position called "TEAM Evangelism" also has a valid scriptural interpretation. It not only fits Scripture but also fits the personalities of all Christians, not just one group. This position recognizes individuals, acknowledging that some Christians are without complexes: people who know no fear, people who can use any method under any situation, with anyone, and win them to Christ. It recognizes that a method suitable to this personality would be "beyond the scope" of the average Christian. It recognizes that few people have the above outstanding qualities. It also recognizes that most Christians are timid, and an

89

attempt at direct Confrontational Evangelism is an overwhelming experience for them.

THE POSITION OF TEAM EVANGELISM

Team Evangelism recognizes two main groups in the church:

1. God has given to some Christians (it appears to be approximately 10%)[1] the gift of Evangelism, which endows them to be effective and confrontational while leading people to Christ. This gift can manifest itself through mass evangelism (preaching to groups) or through personal confrontational witnessing one-on-one, pursuing a decision.

2. God at the same time gives *every* Christian the responsibility to be a *witness*.

It is important to recognize here that the largest difference in the functions of the different groups is the methods, not the results of each. Witnesses have the responsibility to take advantage of the opportunities God provides for them to actively present the Gospel, while Evangelists have the responsibility to make the opportunities for themselves. A fine line exists as to what may be called an opportunity. We must allow this decision to be made in the heart of the person being faced with the situation, for he or she alone will be responsible before God as to how he or she used or did not use the situation.

This position does not relieve Christians from reaching out to a lost world with the Gospel, but only acknowledges that God endows some people to do this through methods that may not fit all people.

THE BOTTOM LINE

The bottom line comes in actual practice of the principles, not in their interpretation. Let's take a look at the key principles of Team Evangelism:

1. Every Christian should evangelize in one manner or another.

You can evangelize without being an Evangelist. I remember a young woman in my home church several years ago. The pastor and Evangelist were trying to motivate our members to "go out and win the lost." The woman in my Sunday school class told me, "If they think I'm going to go out and get people saved, they're crazy, because I just can't do it." Yet that very evening, she and her husband were responsible for having 26 visitors in the service. Several of them accepted Christ during the invitation. Was she an Evangelist or not? She didn't think she was. However, she was doing the work of an Evangelist, but not through direct confrontation, which she thought was expected of her.

Witnesses have the responsibility to take advantage of the opportunities God provides for them to actively present the Gospel, while Evangelists have the responsibility to make the opportunities for themselves.

2. God has endowed some Christians with the gift of Evangelism that will enable them, more so than others, to function more effectively within the boundaries of the methods used in the average outreach (or visitation) program. God has not called everyone to be a part of an outreach program. A person God has not called to be a part of it should not have to bear the burden of guilt nor be made to feel unspiritual or inadequate for not practicing that type of evangelism.

Guilt is not always a motivator, but quite often a tool of Satan for destruction. Most guilt only suppresses efficiency. A distinction must be made between the guilt associated with the Holy Spirit convicting one of sin, and the false guilt placed by people when one does not live up to another person's expectations. The guilt from the Holy Spirit is associated with conviction. If the principle being conveyed is not for that person or the teaching is not valid, the Holy Spirit will not convict. One must be careful not to attempt to do the Holy Spirit's work for Him.

As mentioned, studies done in the church growth movement indicate that approximately ten percent of Christians have the gift of Evangelism,[1] suggesting that ninety percent do not have that gift, but have another dominant gift in their lives.

91

3. *Balance needs to be taught when it comes to evangelism.* There is a difference between people and methodology. Help each Christian find where he or she fits in so he or she can effectively help the non-Christian take another step toward making that decision for Christ. One may not be able to directly confront someone with the Gospel and obtain an immediate decision from them, but one person can play a vital part in bringing another person one step closer to accepting Christ.

4. *Understand fear as an excuse.* Fear is a hush-hush subject. It's something we all have; yet we typically don't want anyone else to know. And because others are afraid to mention it, we think they don't have any fear—thus making us believe we are the only ones who do. I took a speech class once. I was surprised with the boldness with which the instructor talked about fear while all the students sat there acting as if they didn't know what he was talking about. All the while they were shaking in their shoes, knowing he was going to call on one of them soon to stand in front of the class and make a speech.

I have a friend who worked for the telephone company. We were riding along in the car one day when he suddenly pointed and said, "See that pole—pole number 628743? I'll never forget that one. It's the one we worked on the first day I worked for the phone company, ten years ago. I was scared to death."

I quickly answered, saying, "You mean they made you climb a telephone pole the first day you worked for them?"

"No," he said. "I was afraid they were going to ask me to."

> *Knowledge brings self-confidence and self-confidence will eradicate much of the fear because of knowing one can face what he or she fears.*

Preaching on fear will never get many amens. The fearless think the preacher is crazy or making excuses for the fearful, and the fearful are too afraid to shout "Amen."

In Revelation 21:8 the fearful are listed as the number one inhabitants of Hell—those who were scared to profess faith in Christ for fear of ridicule or of what others would think. Fear is not something that can be preached away. This usually leads to frustration on the part of the fearful party. The presence of fear must be equally balanced with understanding and practical application, or "how to" type teaching, in order to overcome fear. Knowledge brings self-confidence and self-confidence will eradicate much of the fear because of knowing one can face what he or she fears.

Therefore, TEAM Evangelism stresses that every Christian, both new and old, should take an active part in a personal evangelism training class. Thoughtful instructors can train without scaring the students to death or putting them in embarrassing situations.

This training can do two things for the church:

a) Those who do not have the gift of Evangelism will soon learn how to be a better witness. Yet, the practical teaching will help them overcome much of their fear. This makes it easier for them to *witness* to others while they minister in another capacity; using the gift God has given them.

b) Those who have the gift of Evangelism will soon develop a stronger burden for winning the lost. I am convinced that no one can sit through practical teaching about the gift God has given him or her without soon getting a burden from God with the conviction and motivation to exercise that gift.

c) Fear may still be present after the training, but God will give the motivation needed to overcome it.

5. Perhaps the greatest hindrance to witnessing is lack of discipline.

Christians must *force* themselves to carry out the responsibilities of their gifts and the duty to witness. They must form habits that place them in the opportunities that best suit their gifts and abilities. When they fail to take advantage of opportunities where the freedom of the Holy Spirit to witness is evident, they develop a pattern of missed opportunities. Proper training in an effective evangelism class or workshop will help to set those practices and the self-discipline necessary to be the most effective.

HOW TO REACH OUR FRIENDS AND RELATIVES

Especially since the early 90s, much has been written on reaching "Seekers," also sometimes called "pre-Christians." Since Bill Hybels made the term Seekers popular more than twenty years ago, pastors and church growth experts have explored numerous strategies from seeker-targeted to seeker-sensitive churches. We have explored the minds of non-churched Harry and Mary, revamped our nurseries, changed our music, updated our sermons, digitalized our sanctuaries, put our content online, and restructured our worship services to be more appealing and inviting to non-Christians seeking answers to spiritual fulfillment. These approaches to restructuring are good. They have helped us reach many people for Christ whom we would not have reached otherwise.

These Seekers we so desperately try to reach are people who are looking to fill the spiritual void in their lives, longing for a spiritual experience, or pursuing "spiritual" (not necessarily biblical or Christian) solutions on how to cope in an overly complex and out-of-control world. Most are unsaved, but some are Christians seeking a more rewarding and fulfilling spiritual experience.

Stop for a moment and think of some of the people who you would love to see come to Christ. If you will, write the names of the top seven people you would like to see reached for Christ on the lines below. Read on for a greater understanding of how to influence them toward salvation.

1. _____
2. _____
3. _____
4. _____
5. _____
6. _____
7. _____

While we recognize that Seekers may be Christians or non-Christians, *all non-saved or non-churched people are* not *Seekers.* An overwhelming majority are non-Seekers—those who don't really give a rip about spiritual things and would rather you not bring them up either. In fact, *most of the people we really wish we could reach for Christ are non-Seekers.* To evaluate this claim for yourself, go back to your list of seven people you would like to see reached for Christ. Notice how many are Seekers and how many are non-Seekers. If you are like most Christians, eighty percent or more of the names on your list are non-Seekers.

So what's the point? *Seeker-oriented methodology won't work for reaching or—as far as that goes—influencing non-Seekers in today's culture.* Stop and think for a minute of the methods we have used to reach people for Christ in the past two generations. The most recent methods of restructuring our churches to make them more "user friendly" or seeker-sensitive (e.g. technological additions such as large screens, improved audio-visual presentations, etc.) are probably the first to come to mind. But consider the more widely known methods that we don't even think of as being attractive to Seekers—like citywide crusades or revival meetings.

Who comes to these events? Mostly Christians, but other attendees who are not Christians are Seekers, looking for answers to life's ultimate questions. Now think about the traditional weeknight visitation program that has been the backbone of Christian outreach in America for the past century. Such visitation strategies have focused on non-members, typically Seekers, who visited our church on Sunday morning. On the other hand, look at the program that has probably trained more people in personal evangelism than any other in the past several decades: *Evangelism Explosion* (EE), started by Dr. D. James Kennedy in 1962. You might say EE is not a Seeker-oriented approach. True, *but it only works with Seekers.* Today's Non-Seekers are incapable of relating to its simple presentation. *Most* methods of evangelism that have worked in the past are not working today. The culture has changed but our basic approach has not.

> While we recognize that Seekers may be Christians or non-Christians, all non-saved or non-churched people are not Seekers.

Have you ever heard the expression, "You can't get a man saved until you get him lost"? Well, you cannot get a non-Seeker "saved" until you turn him or her into a Seeker. Non-Seekers lack the mental environment for accepting the Gospel. Therefore, we must change the environment in which they think. To do this we must build trusting relationships with them.

If I want my non-churched friend to believe in Christ and attend my church, then I must get my friend to establish a trusting relationship with as many of my churched friends as possible.

Trusting relationships are the key to reaching people for Christ and bonding them to His church. Research done by church growth experts Win and Charles Arn shows that the more relationships an individual has within the church, the more apt that individual is to stay in the church. And conversely, the fewer relationships an individual has in the church, the less apt that individual is to stay in the church. O. J. Bryson calls it "the rule of seven: When a church member has seven close friends in a church, he or she will never leave it."

Elmer Towns says, "Relationships are the glue that make people stick to the church." In essence, the more relationships non-Seekers have with those who attend church, the greater the chance the non-Seeker will become more receptive to the Gospel. Thus, if I want my non-churched friend to believe in Christ and attend my church, then I must get my friend to establish a trusting relationship with as many of my churched friends as possible.

Here's a different way of looking at it. To influence your friend for Christ there are a number of potentially influential relationships at work, some existing and some non-existing. The first is the existing relationship between you and your non-churched friend or relative. The second is your relationship with Christ. The third is your relationship with the members of your church.

However, there is no relation between your friends and the members who make up your church. In reality, probably a number of barriers exist between your non-churched friend and the church. Things like, "They're just a bunch of hypocrites." Or, "They just want your money." Or, "Christians are intolerant." Our goal is to go around these barriers and develop a third relationship, one between my friend and my church members.

AMEs AND RSAs?

Here's how Red Lion Evangelical Free Church (Jamie Swalm, Jr. Pastor) in Delaware uses small groups to reach non-Seekers. The tool is *relationship* teams; the application is called *AMEs* and *RSAs*:

> **AMEs:** *Acquaintance Making Events.* An AME is an event for the purpose of introducing non-saved and non-churched friends to other church members. These events usually take place in larger groups (8 plus), never one on one, and are more formal than not in the sense that they are planned and organized ahead of time. AMEs are social gatherings, picnics, cookouts, parties, hospitality events, afternoon teas, etc. They usually take place outside the church. Their purpose is simple: to help develop a three-way relationship or friendship bridge between you, the non-saved or non-churched friend you invite, and the regular members of the group.
>
> AMEs are perfect for helping existing church members develop caring, receptive, redemptive, trusting relationships with outsiders when we remember four basic rules:
>
> 1. Be sure to invite your non-saved and non-churched friends every time your group has a *social* function. Most people don't come because we don't invite them. We tend to socialize with the same crowd all the time and forget those outside our comfort zone.
>
> 2. Be sensitive to who your friends are. Don't get too churchy or too pushy. AMEs are not for presenting the Gospel, but for *creating an environment for accepting the Gospel.* These functions are far less threatening to the non-Seeker when held outside the church.
>
> 3. Be sure to mingle and do not ignore the newcomers at social functions. We have a tendency to spend all our time socializing with those we already know and ignore all strangers, beyond being introduced to them. If they feel ignored or don't make new friends they won't come back. Make an extra effort to include them.

97

4. Be patient. It takes time (sometimes years) to develop relationships that are strong enough for outsiders to feel comfortable with new people. As they become comfortable with your church friends, they will also be more comfortable and receptive to the message of the Gospel. Don't give up on your friends. Keep inviting them, even if they do give excuses for why they can't come "this time."

RSAs: *Relationship Strengthening Activities.* RSAs are any activity for the purpose of developing, cultivating, strengthening, and building trusting relationships between your non-churched friends and other church members. These activities usually take place in smaller groups (four or less) or one on one and are more informal in the sense that they are less planned and more spontaneous.

After you have met and become acquainted with new people at the AMEs, practice RSAs—involve them in your daily activities, *just like you do with any friend.* Get their email addresses and phone numbers and invite them out to dinner, or invite them to your home for dinner or dessert. Take them fishing or to a ball game with you. Ask them to go shopping with you. Or, just call them and say, "I'm going to the hardware store, do you need anything or would you like to ride along?"

My wife and her friend, Fran, host a "Make-it, Take-it" night at our house once a week. They invite a group of ladies over to do crafts. (They *make it* and *take it* home the same night.) They have brief devotions and prayer before their mid-meeting refreshments. The rest of the time is spent making crafts and getting to know one another. The key to RSAs is to spend time with people to cultivate the relationship. Here again we need to observe a few simple rules:

1. Don't be on the edge of your seat all evening looking for the perfect time to twist the conversation into a presentation of the Gospel. If the opportunity or question arises, take advantage of it. If it doesn't, don't worry about it. Just relax and enjoy each other's company.

Remember, the goal is not to present the Gospel as quickly as possible, but to create an environment for accepting the Gospel when it is presented, whether by you or someone else.

2. Be a good witness. Avoid questionable activities such as R-rated or in some cases even inappropriate PG-13 movies. Don't take your friends any place you wouldn't take Jesus.

3. Don't condemn or belittle your friend's lifestyle. If you go to a restaurant and your friend drops an F-bomb, don't get hyper; just change the subject and go on with the evening. If your friend is living with open sin, don't make an issue of it. Don't discuss politics. Who knows, your friend may have voted for the guy you think is a jerk. Let the Lord deal with these issues after the person becomes a Christian.

As mentioned earlier, trust is a very important factor in cultivating these relationships and bonding with people. Charles Handy, in *The Hungry Spirit* (Broadway Books, 1998), lists seven principles of trust. Keep these principles in mind when dealing with non-Seekers:

1. "Trust is not blind." To trust someone is to know them. AMEs and RSAs provide an environment conducive to building relationships and trust. In these regular get-togethers, people get to know one another better.

2. "Trust needs boundaries." There are boundaries we cannot cross in getting to know people. We must not be nosy and must be careful of the questions we ask acquaintances. Typically, the more time you spend with someone, the more comfortable you both will be in sharing thoughts and feelings with one another.

> *The goal is not to present the Gospel as quickly as possible, but to create an environment for accepting the Gospel when it is presented, whether by you or someone else.*

3. "Trust requires constant learning." We must be open to new ideas and ways to strengthen relationships. We should look for opportunities to learn from our mistakes—and know when to take action or speak, and when not to do so.

4. "Trust is tough." Gaining someone's trust takes time and effort. Trust is hard to regain once broken. Be careful how you use the information you know about someone else; take care not to offend them nor pass on personal information to others in the form of a gossipy "prayer request."

5. "Trust needs bonding." We must be willing to spend time with others in different environments—in fun activities outside the church as well as activities inside the church.

6. "Trust needs touch." In other words, we need to make people feel special. We need to invest time in their lives and have genuine concern for them—and prove it through our actions.

7. "Trust has to be earned." We must be consistent in our "walk" and "talk." We must prove ourselves worthy of trust.

The key to AMEs and RSAs is to create receptivity in the mind of the non-Seeker by building a bridge between the Gospel and their non-Christian foundation. In its truest sense, this form of reaching out to others is TEAM Evangelism. Individual Christians are no longer charged to go it alone to fulfill the Great Commission. The group works together as a TEAM to support each other, pray for their lost friends, and especially to create the environment of friendship that is needed to bond newcomers with a lasting relationship to Christ and His church. If you want to reach the Seekers *and the non-Seekers* in your sphere of influence, I challenge you put together TEAMS and encourage the use of AMEs and RSAs in your own church. Remember most

If you want to reach the Seekers and the non-Seekers in your sphere of influence, I challenge you put together TEAMS and encourage the use of AMEs and RSAs in your own church.

100

people who are non-Christians are also non-Seekers. And the best way to turn non-Seekers into Seekers is through the influence of trusting relationships.

NEXT STEPS

Nowhere does the value of God's plan for spiritual gifts come into focus more than in the total process of evangelism and outreach. The guilt must be removed from those who are serving God in their gifted areas. Again, teamwork is essential in order to be most effective. In this area more than possibly any other, Christians have been guilty of "gift imposing". Guilt has been imposed on those who do not live up to the expectations of someone else. It is difficult to live up to what God expects, but it is ten times more difficult to live up to what others often expect. God equips people to live to His expectations, not in other people's expectations.

Different people have taken different approaches to evangelism because of their backgrounds or spiritual gifts and the influences on their lives. Believers need to realize that if God has not gifted them in certain areas, they should not force themselves to be what they are not, but to work as God has gifted them. Then believers must TEAM up with those of differing gifts so they can *together* reach this generation with the Gospel, win them to Christ, and teach them how to mature and grow into a complete Christian. Individual believers can be more effective by being themselves than by trying to be someone else.

The church must evangelize! Every believer must become involved somewhere in the process of evangelizing, as part of the TEAM. In other words, your spiritual gift may relieve you from the responsibility of Confrontational Evangelism, but it will never relieve you from the responsibility to evangelize.

101

FOR PERSONAL REFLECTION

1. Describe "Workforce Economics."

2. What are the three positions on evangelism?

3. What is the key to the TEAM Evangelism position as outlined?

4. How has the "confrontation" method of witnessing affected your own ministry? Which of the three positions would make you most comfortable? Why?

5. How can people overcome the greatest hindrance to witnessing?

6. How are the definitions of witnessing affecting you and what changes does the new definition bring to mind for you?

FOR GROUP DISCUSSION

1. There are only _____ groups responsible for doing evangelism.

_____

_____

2. The key to reaching people for Christ is . . .

_____

3. The method is_____

Review your list of seven people you want to reach for Christ (p. 99)

1. _____
2. _____
3. _____
4. _____
5. _____
6. _____
7. _____

4. The dominant philosophy and method of evangelism for the past twenty years is:

_____

But, the people we *really* want to reach for Christ are:

_____

5. Seeker-oriented _____ won't work
for reaching or influencing non-Seekers in today's culture.

Non-Seekers lack a _____.

We must create an _____

for the _____ *of the Gospel.*

6. We must develop _____ relationships.

The goal is to develop as many strong relationships with as many people in the church without coercing or pressuring the individual.

7. Developing 3-way (bonding) relationships.

AMEs_____

Event held for the purpose of introducing unsaved and unchurched friends of church members to other church members.

Usually larger groups; never one-on-one; more formal.

8. RSAs_____

Any activity for the purpose of developing, cultivating and strengthening relationships between unchurched friends of church members and other church members.

Usually smaller groups; one-on-one; more informal.

103

Note: Answers for each chapter's "For Group Discussion" questions can be found on pages 183-184

WHEN SPIRITUAL GIFTS ARE MISUSED
OR ABUSED, THEY DO NOT MEET THE
NEEDS OF PEOPLE IN THE FAMILY OF
GOD. OFTEN, THE TEAM PULLS APART
RATHER THAN PULLING TOGETHER. IF WE
UNDERSTAND THE ABUSES THAT CAN
TAKE PLACE, WE CAN AVOID THEM AND
CONCENTRATE OUR EFFORTS ON THE
TASK GOD GAVE US.

ABUSING THE TEAM GIFTS

The great violinist Nicolo Paganini thrilled audiences with his musical performances. His violin was the source of melodies and harmonies impossible to describe in words. What joys the violin conveyed in the hands of the master. When he died, he willed his expensive and beautiful violin to the city of Genoa. The only condition was that it was never to be played again. The wood, since it was never used, decayed and became worm-eaten and useless. That beautifully toned instrument was grossly abused instead of providing the melodic tones for which it was intended. The same choice comes to Christians with their spiritual gifts—they can use their gifts or abuse them. The results are much the same as with Paganini's violin: spiritual gifts add beauty to life when used properly, or sadness and uselessness when left alone.

God intended for spiritual gifts to be used in carrying out the Great Commission and edifying the saints. When spiritual gifts are misused or abused, they do not meet the needs of people in the family of God. Often, the TEAM pulls apart rather than pulling together. If we understand the abuses that can take place, we can avoid them and concentrate our efforts on the task God gave us. Let's look at some terms that describe the misuses of spiritual gifts.

GIFT IGNORANCE

In 1 Corinthians 12:1, Paul writes, "Now concerning spiritual gifts, brethren, I would not have you ignorant" (KJV). Today when we call someone *ignorant* we insinuate they are stupid, a fool, or illiterate, but when Paul used the term in this passage he simply meant *a lack of knowledge.* Just like in Paul's days, ignorance or lack of knowledge is the number one problem plaguing spiritual gifts today. I must reinforce here that the problem goes far beyond simply knowing what an individual's spiritual gifts are.

Many Christians can tell you the name of their spiritual gift, but few really understand the principles that revolve around the gifts. They are eager to identify their dominant gift, but are left wondering what to do with it. For example, as of 2014, the *Your Gifts* Spiritual Gifts Survey had more than 5,000,000 users while the text that explains its application had sold less then 100,000 copies. This still leaves many ignorant of spiritual gifts.

Ignorance of spiritual gifts may be the major cause of much of the discouragement, insecurity, frustration and guilt that plagues many Christians and holds back the church's effectiveness and growth.

Gift Ignorance is a lack of knowledge regarding the possession of spiritual gifts and their function. This lack of knowledge has evolved over the centuries from historical absence to modern abstinence. Whereas the forefathers gave us little material to study, the contemporary scholars have not addressed the task-oriented (Team) gifts in their studies of the Holy Spirit.

Most contemporary scholars do agree that the doctrine of the Holy Spirit is one of the most important doctrines of Christianity. Churches lacking a sound scriptural teaching on this doctrine will also have problems on other doctrines as well. Yet historians seem to verify that the doctrine has been under attack ever since the beginning of the Ante-Nicene period (AD 100) and almost totally suppressed during the Dark and Middle Ages (approximately 450-1517). John Walvoord states:

> "The Middle Ages on the whole were dark spiritually as well as intellectually, with few attaining any balance of doctrine acceptable to the earnest Bible student of today. Of the doctrine of the Holy Spirit in its entirety, there was practically no conception. Few grasped the need for personal conversion and the work of the Spirit in regeneration. Practically no attention was given to such subjects as the indwelling Spirit, the baptism of the Spirit, and the filling of the Spirit. It was expressly denied that the Spirit could teach all

106

Christians through the Word of God. Earthly priests were substitut-ed for the Holy Spirit. The 'things of the Spirit of God' were lost in the wilderness of sacramentarianism (salvation through the taking of sacraments), ignorance of the Word, superstition, humanism and scholasticism."[1]

Beginning with the Reformation in the early 16th century, things began to change with Martin Luther's emphasis on the Spirit's work in regeneration and illumina-tion, and John Calvin's teachings on the association of the Spirit and the Trinity. Other great contributions included John Owen's *Discourse Concerning the Holy Spirit* and Abraham Kuyper's *The Work of the Holy Spirit*. Kuyper's work was pub-lished in 1900, beginning this century's writings on the subject. Most of the works before 1900 said almost nothing about the gifts of the Spirit, or listed the gifts with no theological *or* practical definition for them. Between 1900 and 1950, no practical application was given.

Dr. Robert Lightner, Professor Emeritus of Systematic Theology at Dallas Theological Seminary, summed it up best when he said, "Perhaps the most ne-glected area of the doctrine of the Holy Spirit has been the ministry of giving gifts to the members of Christ's body."[2]

Most modern attention to gifts of the Holy Spirit has mainly centered on the "Miraculous Gifts," such as healing, tongues, and miracles, with very little—if any—emphasis on the TEAM Gifts (task-oriented gifts). Although revival of the doctrine of spiritual gifts has been evident in this recent period, the abstinence of its application still remains.

GIFT BLINDNESS

Gift Blindness results from gift ignorance and renders victims incapable of rec-ognizing their own spiritual gifts and the influence of gifts on their own life and ministry.

An experience while on vacation with my family in the Pocono Mountains helped me see this clearly. My son-in-law and I wanted to go fishing. But being from out of state, we needed to get Pennsylvania fishing licenses. We went to this little country store that sold everything from groceries to hardware and fishing licenses. We walked to the counter in the back corner where a young lady proceeded to ask a number of questions while she filled out an application, including name, height, weight, etc.

When she got to color of eyes, I said, "I don't know, what color are they?" as I leaned over the counter so she could get a closer look.

She said, "Yellow."

"Yellow," I said, "My eyes aren't yellow."

"With those sunglasses, they are," she replied.

Sure enough, I had completely forgotten that I was wearing my clip-on sunglasses. I had even commented to my son-in-law that it was a little dark when we entered the store. But I had been wearing them so long that I totally forgot that they were influencing the way I saw things. In fact, I thought everyone was seeing my surroundings the same as I was.

The same is true with spiritual gifts. Many times those who are ignorant of spiritual gifts fail to see that they are looking at the world through the eyes of the gifts that God has given them. They think that everyone else should be looking at the world in the same way. They suffer from *gift blindness*.

Those afflicted with *gift blindness* may demonstrate a tendency to build doctrine around themselves, interpret Scripture in light of their own feelings or emotions, and adjust their lifestyle to fulfill their personal desires. They are blind to the fact that their own emotions, desires, motivation and motives are influenced by their own gift. They become theo-methodologists (i.e., the methodology that gives *them* fulfillment in life has become their theology).

Theo-methodologists are often guilty of Bible manipulation. Once their position is established, much effort is made to find verses that support it. This is the opposite of the proper procedure of studying the Scripture, then establishing a position. In reality, theo-methodologists build doctrines around themselves.

Years ago, I worked in the sign business. Tony, another man who had been in the sign business, lived near me. I was excited about what I was doing and could not understand why Tony was not excited about it any more. Every time I was around Tony, I tried to talk him into going back into the sign business. I still could not see why he was not as excited as I was about what excited me.

We are often like that about our spiritual gifts. Our own spiritual gifts and the characteristics and desires related to those gifts excite us. People who do not have the same gifts may not be as excited about the same ministry areas.

Gift blindness sometimes takes that form; it does not see the gifts that others have and how they too work for the glory of God. We must not be blind to our own gifts; we must not be blind to the gifts of others.

Some people tend to "beat people with the Bible" because others disagree with their positions. The trend is to consider those who have other gifts to be less spiritual.

The following diagram ("The Value of Needs As Seen By the Nine Different Team Gifts") shows the importance that is put on the various areas of the ministry by the various members of the body. This emphasis is influenced by the motivation and desires resulting from different spiritual gifts. When people are blind to the fact that their spiritual gifts provide such an influence on their life, they may create much frustration by taking the most positive drives of their spiritual gifts and *imposing* them on others.

109

THE VALUE OF NEEDS AS SEEN BY THE NINE DIFFERENT TEAM GIFTS

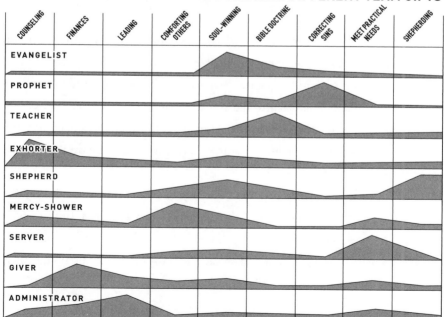

GIFT IMPOSING

Gift Imposing is the act of forcing one's spiritual gift upon another and attempting to compel them to perform as though it were God's gift to them. Gift imposing wants the whole body to be an eye.

Gift imposing is nothing new. Paul dealt with it with the Corinthians. It appeared that those with different gifts were not welcome. But Paul reinforces the necessity of all the gifts to complete the body:

> *Even so the body is not made up of one part but of many. Now if the foot should say, "Because I am not a hand, I do not belong to the body," it would not for that reason stop being part of the body. And if the ear should say, "Because I am not an eye, I do not belong to the body," it would not for that reason stop being part of the body. If the whole body were an eye, where would the sense of hearing be? If the whole body were an ear, where would the sense of smell be? But in fact God has placed the parts in the body, every one of them, just as he wanted them to be. If they were all one part, where would the body be? As it is, there are many parts, but one body. The eye cannot say to the hand, "I don't need you!" And the head cannot say to the feet, "I don't need you!"* (1 Corinthians 12:14-21).

What the Corinthians were saying: "If you don't have the same gifts as us we don't need you, because you're not as valuable as we are."

Gift imposing is most frequently practiced by those who suffer from gift blindness. Such individuals fail to recognize the diversity of the body of Christ and, as a result, attempt to force other Christians to function in capacities for which God has not gifted them. Because of their blindness they think everyone sees the world as they do.

Gift imposers give the impression that they believe the area of ministry for which God has gifted and burdened them is superior to all others. In fact, some not only give the impression, but they "know" their gifts are the only ones that count—perhaps even the only ones in existence. "Gift imposers" distribute much frustration, discouragement, and false guilt on others in the body of Christ.

Gift imposing involves "guilt-trip motivation" in imposing gifts on others. People who practice it try to make others feel that they are not right with God unless they are involved with the same ministry as they are. For example, a person may have the gift of Evangelism. He is motivated and consumed with personally leading people to Christ. He or she witnesses through blog posts, social media discussions, talking to people on the street, in doctor's offices, or just anywhere and any time he or she can.

No believer who uses his or her gift properly should feel guilty for not having the same gift someone else has been given.

Then this Evangelist finds a fellow Christian who has the gift of Serving or Mercy-Showing. Since the person is not out on the streets "shaking the bushes" and confronting every person he or she comes in contact with, the Evangelist accuses the person of not being burdened about the lost. In reality, that may be far from the truth. The Mercy-Shower may have been responsible for many coming to Christ because of his or her special ministry. The Server may have opened doors the Evangelist could only wish to open.

No believer who uses his or her gift properly should feel guilty for not having the same gift someone else has been given.

In the church, gift imposers "impose" in two basic ways: first, with and because of the burden of their own hearts; second, with the one string banjo, where week in and week out, the same message is restated and presented again. This drives many away and makes the ones who stay think that all there is to ministry is the one thing continuously emphasized.

GIFT GRAVITATION

Gift Gravitation refers to the tendency among Christians to attract and be attracted to other Christians with like spiritual gifts. It grows out of the natural tendency of individuals to form bonds with those of like interests and aspirations (the Homogeneous Unit). Certainly, there is nothing wrong with fellowship with others and exchanging ideas and plans for using our gifts, but we must be careful not to form cliques and exclude those with differing gifts.

111

GIFT COLONIZATION

Gift Colonization is the direct and inescapable result of unrestrained gift gravitation. Gift gravitation is perfectly normal and a result of human nature and the need to be accepted by those who are similar to us (our peers). Gift colonization is the extreme result of gift gravitation, wherein we isolated ourselves from the rest of the church in many ways. The real problem comes with our failure to recognize that we are colonizing, and then attacking those who are not the same as we are.

Gift gravitation is the *process* usually practiced by laypeople, and gift colonization is the *result*, which is usually unwittingly sustained by the leaders.

When it comes to colonization, possibly the strongest magnetism drawing people together are values. Spiritual gifts influence values, which in turn lead people with those gifts to gravitate toward one another. However, in most cases, those guilty of gift colonization have only a superficial awareness of spiritual gifts and their function (gift ignorance).

The negative result of colonization is that many pastors quit preaching *to* their congregations, and start preaching *at* the congregation down the street or on the other side of town (or the nation). Once colonization takes place it is easier to preach at the other guy. Every Sunday morning the sermon is not what this church should be doing, but what the other church, or group of churches (movement) should not be doing. This causes the pastor's own congregation to feel cozy, self-righteous, and complacent.

Over the years, there has been increasing evidence of gift colonization in the major church movements in America. Careful observation of these movements reveals that their characteristics, strengths, weaknesses, ministry emphases, and leadership styles correlate with the characteristics of certain spiritual gifts. Such correlation leads to accepting doctrines and philosophies that support those characteristics, therefore making their colonization even stronger. Spiritual gifts are a major factor in the indeliberate formation of the individual movements. There are many similarities among all the movements. This does not mean that everyone in each movement has the same gift. On the contrary, all gifts are present in each movement, but certain spiritual gifts are more evident and have become dominant in each movement. Every movement is not guilty of gift colonization; however, when carried to excess, such trends are evident.

When someone within a movement has a particular gift that is not part of the gift colonization for that movement, they are forced to either gravitate to another movement or misuse their gift. For example, a person with the gift of Evangelism who is in a non-evangelistic movement may proselytize in order to fulfill the motivation of his or her gift. The lack of an evangelistic emphasis within his or her own movement may spur the Evangelist to recruit churched people to their movement's philosophy rather than bringing lost people to Christ.

GIFT COLONIZATION AS SEEN IN MAJOR MOVEMENTS

MOVEMENT	MINISTRY EMPHASIS	DOMINANT GIFTS	STRENGTHS	WEAKNESSES	LEADERSHIP STYLE
Fundamentalist	Soul Winning Preaching Purity Visitation	Evangelism Prophecy Administration	Strong Outreach Local Church Politically Conservative Organization	Drift Legalistic Impose Guilt Sporadic Lean Militant Theomethod-ologists	Authoritative Pastor Leads
Evangelical	Bible teaching Academics Organization	Teaching Administration	Strong Bible Teaching Organization Bible Exposition	Over-emphasis on Intellectual Lack of Practical Content Oriented Weak Evange-lism	Pastor Teaches
Deep Life	Personal Edification	Exhortation	Applied Theology Discipleship Unity Tolerance	Non-Evangelistic Self-centered Collectors of Unsatisfied Sheep, Lack Organization	Pastor Shepherds Flock Feeds Flock
Charismatic	Compassion Experience Worship	Mercy-Showing	Sensitivity to the Holy Spirit Meets Emotional Needs	Emotionalism Universal Church Proselyte Feeling Oriented	Involved Leader (Coach)
Church Growth	Church Planting Evangelism Assimilation Discipleship Methods Balance	Exhortation Administration Teaching	Evangelistic Nurture Organized Pioneer's Spirit Scientific	Formulation Non-dependent on the Holy Spirit Pragmatic Methodology	Visionary Pastor Leads
Liberal (Within the bounds of Christianity)	Social Oriented Humanitarian	Shepherd Server Giver	Meets Social Needs Meets Physical Needs	No Evangelism Declining Growth Tend to teach distorted Gospel Compromise	Pastor Ministers to Congregation Maintenance

113

Here's the positive and the negative of what happens when a whole local church is dominant in a particular gift, but over-emphasizes that gift to the exclusion of others.

Evangelists - tend to build *soul-winning* churches; many converts, but many become "back-door" churches where people are saved, but leave the church for lack of discipleship.

Prophets - tend to build *discerning* churches: awareness of sin, close monitoring of behavior, tend to become "legalistic."

Teachers - tend to build *doctrinally strong* churches; deep theological studies, content oriented, but weak on application.

Exhorters - tend to build *deeper-life* churches; emphasis on personal edification and application, shallow outreach and doctrine.

Shepherds - tend to build *caring* churches; a lot of shepherding, follow-up, and care taking, but oriented toward maintenance of congregation.

Givers - tend to build *mission-oriented* churches, home and foreign support raised, strong giving, overemphasis of money.

Mercy-Showers - tend to build *affectionate* churches; tears and smiles, hugs, prayer, praise worship, overly emotional.

Servers - tend to build *humanitarian* churches; community awareness, help poor and underprivileged, neglects the spiritual.

Administrators - tend to build *well-organized* churches, many programs, many committees, but may lack spiritual and doctrinal depth.

GIFT COVETING

Gift coveting is the activity of desiring a gift other than that which has been given to the individual by the Holy Spirit. This will lead to frustration and a lack of fulfillment since God's true purpose for the individual is never achieved.

Mercy-Showers should not wish for the gift of Evangelism, but should use the gift they have to touch and soften hearts. Prophets should not wish for the gift of Serving so that they would be better liked. Let Servers keep the building in good repair so Prophets can spend time in prayer, Bible study and preaching. Let every one carry their part of the load and allow the other people to carry their share.

Many times Christians waste their lives wishing they were someone else. God knew who could be trusted with which gifts, so He placed them in the proper hands. First Corinthians 12:18 says, "But in fact God has placed the parts in the body, every one of them, just as he wanted them to be." John 15:16 states, "You did not choose me, but I chose you and appointed you so that you might go and bear fruit—fruit that will last—and so that whatever you ask in my name the Father will give you."

Some would argue that in 1 Corinthians 12:31 Paul exhorts us to covet gifts we don't have when he says, "But, covet earnestly the best gifts" (KJV). This could be confusing because without further examination, what Paul has just said in this passage is contradictory to everything he had said in the previous passages. He has just finished saying you are not to covet others' gifts, not to be boastful or wish that you have a gift that you don't have. The best translation I was able to find for this passage was "earnestly desire the higher gifts" (NASB).

Paul had just finished showing us the higher gifts in verse 28. "And God has placed in the church first of all apostles, second prophets, third teachers, then miracles, then gifts of healing, of helping, of guidance, and of different kinds of tongues." So the higher gifts at that time were Apostle, Prophet, Teachers and then into the miraculous gifts which some don't believe exist today. So what are the higher task-oriented gifts? They are: *Evangelist, Prophet, Teacher,* and *Exhorter.*

Note that these four gifts minister to the spiritual needs of the people, while the remaining five minister to the physical and emotional needs of the people. Why then is it proper to covet, or desire, these four gifts? Are they the more glamorous gifts that a Christian should want?

Many times Christians waste their lives wishing they were someone else. God knew who could be trusted with which gifts, so He placed them in the proper hands.

115

First we need to understand that Paul is not talking to the individual Christian, but to the church cooperatively. This entire letter was addressed to the church at Corinth (1 Cor. 1:2, "To the church of God in Corinth"). The church itself should desire these four higher gifts because these four gifts are the ones that separate the church from the social club. Remove those four gifts, look at the remaining gifts and see if you don't agree that the American Legion, and all other social clubs have a secular form of the lower gifts. However, they don't have any form of the higher gifts because they have no need to minister to the spiritual needs of their people as the church has.

Why does the corner coffee shop do so well when you have to pay $3 for a medium latte, when for $8 you can buy a whole bag of coffee, take it home and drink coffee for days? Because of fellowship.

You might question, does the VFW, American Legion, or the Lion's Club have a Shepherd? They don't have a pastor in the sense we think of pastors, but most of these clubs will have a person who will meet the basic needs that the pastor does. Usually they will have one person who is sold out for their organization, and works hard caring for the people who are in their club. Social clubs are loaded with *servers*. Women and men will stay there till 3 o'clock in the morning cleaning up after a party.

116

We think as Christians that we have the market cornered on *giving*. We give and tithe, but Christians don't have the corner on the giving market. Non-Christians give too. They have *Administrators*. They always have someone leading and keeping things organized. *Mercy-showing and fellowship* are the largest reasons for their existence. Why does the corner coffee shop do so well when you have to pay $3 for a medium latte, when for $8 you can buy a whole bag of coffee, take it home and drink coffee for days? Because of fellowship. Friends get together. It's meeting a need in their lives.

What do the social clubs lack? They lack the *Evangelists*. There is nobody getting saved in social clubs. They lack the *Prophets*. The last thing you would want in a social club would be someone going around pointing out your sins. They don't need a *Teacher* to explain doctrine. They don't need an

Exhorter trying to change things. They bank heavily on tradition and don't like change. Social clubs are always concerned with your physical, social or emotional needs, but rarely will you meet someone who is interested in your spiritual needs. *If your church lacks the higher gifts, it may be a social club too.*

HOW TO AVOID ABUSES

The best deterrent to abusing spiritual gifts is *education*. Christians must not suffer from gift ignorance. Pastors must teach and preach the whole counsel of God in the area of spiritual gifts.

Three areas of education are needed. First, Christians must be educated concerning what is a spiritual gift. Second, they must be educated concerning what are their own spiritual gifts. Third, they must be educated concerning what are other Christians' spiritual gifts, and how these relate to their own gifts. Then, they must learn how this all fits into the biblical concept of TEAM Ministry.

Spiritual gifts education must combat gift ignorance in believers by covering the first two areas (what a gift is and what their gifts are). Gift blindness is avoided by teaching concerning other Christians' gifts. Gift imposing is an extreme of this blindness when believers not only misuse their own gifts, but force others to function within the wrong gift capacity. By teaching the balance of the body as taught in 1 Corinthians 12, Romans 12 and Ephesians 4:16, gift imposing can be avoided.

Remember that gift gravitation is perfectly natural until it becomes extreme, especially to the point of colonization. This extreme can be avoided by teaching the necessity of having all the gifts in the church so the church as a body can meet the needs of the community and the local church body. Gift coveting is avoided when believers know their gifts and properly function within the body with those gifts. When believers are fulfilled serving in a position that utilizes their own gifts in the church, they have no desire for someone else's gift.

117

When believers are fulfilled serving in a position that utilizes their own gifts in the church, they have no desire for someone else's gift.

NEXT STEPS

When the TEAM Gifts are abused or misused, the entire body of the church suffers. The balance is lost and the work of God is adversely affected. To carry any strength to an extreme is to make it a weakness. All of the abuses are simply strengths carried to an extreme, through "riding a hobby horse" or through a lack of understanding that God did not want everybody to be the same and have the same gifts. God makes everyone different on the outside (some tall, some short; some skinny, some stout; some blonde, brunette or redhead; some dark-skinned, some light-skinned; etc.) and the inside (some Prophets, some Evangelists, some Administrators, some Mercy-Showers, etc. with the various desires and motives characteristic of those gifts). It is easier to recognize the outer differences than the inner differences. Just as we do not belittle a person who is 5'2" for not wearing a size 48-long coat, we should not criticize a Prophet for not being a Mercy-Shower, or any other gifted person for not practicing someone else's gift.

The more Christians mature, the more they will learn to mix with people who have differing gifts and accept their different motives, desires, and needs. They must learn to be part of the TEAM rather than being individuals who must "win the world" on their own. One person does not build a church; one gift does not meet all the needs; one individual does not reach and teach a generation. We must TEAM together and complement each other, realizing the uniqueness of each Christian's giftedness and part in the task God has given.

FOR PERSONAL REFLECTION

1. What is gift imposing and how does it affect God's work?

2. Which abuse can lead to gift blindness if carried to extremes? Why?

3. How do gift gravitation and gift colonization work?

4. What kind of problems would you find in a church with heavy gift colonization? What kind of advantages?

5. Which church in the list of colonized churches would you feel most comfortable in and why?

6. How have you personally suffered as a result of "gift abuses?" What did you learn from the situation? What effect did it have on you and your spiritual life? (Do not use people's names.)

FOR GROUP DISCUSSION

1. Gift _ignorance_

A lack of knowledge regarding the possession of spiritual gifts and the nature of the gifts themselves. The root of all gift abuses.

Evolved from historical absence to modern abstinence.

2. Gift **blindness**

Result of gift ignorance, rendering the victim incapable of recognizing his or her own spiritual gifts and their influence on his or her life and ministry.

May tend to build doctrine around themselves.

May become theo-methodologists—their methodology becomes their theology. Guilty of Bible-manipulation.

May also be blind to the gifts of others.

3. Gift _imposing_

The act of forcing one's spiritual gift upon others, attempting to compel them to perform as though it were God's gift to them.

Tendency to think only their particular gifts really count.

Involves "guilt-trip motivation"—implies others are not right with God unless they are involved with same type of ministry.

Imposing works two ways:

    1. The burden of the heart forced on others.

    2. "One-stringed banjo"—same message restated repeatedly.

119

4. Gift __*gravitation*__

The tendency to attract and be attracted to other Christians with like spiritual gifts.

Homogeneous unit—but be careful of cliques.

5. Gift __*colonization*__

The direct and inescapable result of unrestrained gift gravitation.

The extreme—attacks those who do not have the same gifts.

Gravitation—the process; colonization—the result.

Usually form a church or movement centered on that gift.

6. Gift __*coveting*__

Desiring a gift other than the one given by the Holy Spirit.

Leads to frustration and lack of fulfillment.

Note: Answers for each chapter's "For Group Discussion" questions can be found on pages 183-184

HOW TO DISCOVER
YOUR SPIRITUAL GIFT

S ir Michael Costa, the celebrated conductor, was holding a rehearsal. As the mighty chorus rang out, accompanied by scores of instruments, the piccolo player thought perhaps he could quit playing without being missed since there was so much music in the air at once. Suddenly the great leader stopped and cried out, "Where is the piccolo?" The sound of that one small instrument was necessary for the full harmony of the piece and the conductor's ear had missed it when it did not play. So it is with the individual's spiritual gift. Every part must be played, every gift must be used or the whole will suffer. *You are important!*

We all have heroes in the work of God; people we consider great and outstanding because of their positions and accomplishments. Stop for a moment and think of the most outstanding Christian leader or teacher you know. When you have thought of someone, consider this: God has called you to do something he or she *cannot* do. God has called you to do something that your favorite evangelist can't do, regardless of how great he or she is. Your church needs you in order to fulfill its mission in the community where God placed it. God has called you—"little ole you"—to do something that only you can do. The task may seem small to you, but it is big as far as God is concerned. And just as importantly, that is all God has called you to be accountable for. You will never be called to account for God's calling on someone else's life.

In order to fill that special place in His ministry, you need to know what that special place is. Here are some simple steps to follow.

WHAT *NOT* TO DO

Before we can truly understand what we are *to do*, it would behoove us to look at what we are *not to do*.

Avoid the abuses and misuses of spiritual gifts (see Chapter 7). It is easy to fall into these traps laid by Satan. He has always specialized in causing people to go to extremes with good things and in so doing, cause those good things to become bad. Much of the guilt associated with Christian work is not conviction from the Holy Spirit, but false guilt caused by not living up to the expectations of others. You must make your personal ministry a real matter of prayer, allowing God to reveal to you the real position you occupy in His work.

Don't allow people to impose their gifts on you; don't gravitate or colonize with those with like gifts and become a group of people who do not fit with others who have other gifts; don't be blind to others' gifts; don't be ignorant of your gift nor the gifts of others; don't covet gifts God gave to someone else. He made no mistake when He gave yours to you (see 1 Corinthians 12:18).

Avoid impulsive decisions. Many Bible college and seminary students make the rash mistake of quitting school to become involved in a "more glamorous" ministry, damaging their futures for what seemed to be a great opportunity for serving the Lord. It was an impulsive decision based on feelings and desire more than on God's leadership and plan for success in their lives. They may succeed for a while, but sooner or later, they often become frustrated in their efforts to serve Christ. Many laypeople do the same thing concerning their spiritual gifts. They choose their ministry based on their feelings or some speaker's passionate cry, rather than taking the time to see where they really fit in and what their real gift is.

Don't try to be someone else. Be yourself. I don't want to imply that you cannot serve God without knowing the name of your spiritual gifts. Some people have never heard of spiritual gifts and have been effectively serving God for many years. Yet many suddenly think they have to get a new position to fit their newly found gift. Stop and consider—you might be right where God wants you and you don't need to make any changes whatsoever. *The expression of the gift is more* *important than the title or name.* Make sure your decisions are thought through carefully before you make any changes of ministry.

Avoid "gift obsession." Don't substitute gifts for a Spirit-filled life. Don't make the mistake of making spiritual gifts an end in themselves. They're only a means to an end. This was a problem with the Corinthians, who substituted the Spirit-filled life with spiritual gifts. *A steady diet of any one thing will always cause malnutrition.* Continue studying doctrine, evangelism, church growth principles and, most importantly, the Bible. The key word is *balance* for usefulness in the work of God.

In the relationship of spiritual gifts to God's will, remember the first six principles of the Spirit-filled life: to be saved, sanctified, Spirit-filled, submissive, suffering, and serving.

Another entire study could be done on balance and the priorities that God has set for our lives. I believe that God has five priorities for our lives: *God first* (the foundation on which to build everything else), *family second,* your *ministry third,* your *work fourth,* and *yourself fifth.*

In the relationship of spiritual gifts to God's will, remember the first six principles of the Spirit-filled life: to be *saved, sanctified, Spirit-filled, submissive, suffering,* and *serving.* Serving (the practice of spiritual gifts) is only one part of the Spirit-filled life. We need to be careful not to take gifts out of that perspective.

123

Avoid "gift dodging." In his book *Is My Church What God Meant It To Be?* Gary Hauck writes,

> "Do not neglect other responsibilities by hiding behind your spiritual gift! How often I have heard someone say, 'Oh, no, I don't witness. Evangelism just isn't my spiritual gift!' While it is true that God hasn't given a special unusual ability (or gift) of Evangelism to every Christian, *every Christian* is responsible to evangelize! Paul even told Timothy, who had the gift of Shepherding, to "do the work of an evangelist" (2 Timothy 4:5).
>
> "In the same way, Christians who do not possess the gift of Giving are responsible to uphold the work of God financially, and Christians who do not have the gift of Serving are nevertheless

responsible to 'do good unto all men.' We must not hide behind our spiritual gifts. We are to excel in the area of our gift, but we are not free from responsibility in the other areas of service."[1]

WHAT TO DO

Now that you know what *not* to do, let's take a quick look at how to maximize your gifts.

Learn to perform all the gifts. You might say, "You mean you have taken me this far, through all these distinctions on the gifts, all these separations on the gifts, all these characteristics on the gifts, and now you tell me I have to learn *every one* of them?" Let me explain. Many Scriptures throughout the Bible give you the commands to perform all these functions. Just calling yourself a Christian (Christ-like) implies such a life. Christ is a perfect example of all the gifts and exemplifies the need for you to learn to perform in every gift. But, let's not stop here.

124

Excel in the area of your *dominant* gift. This is the real key in gift usage. Yes, you need to learn to perform all the gifts to an extent. There are times in your life when you will have to confront sin like a Prophet, be practical like an Exhorter, study like a Teacher, confront somebody like a Mercy-Shower, take responsibility as an Administrator, or do service as a Server in the church. You might not like many of these tasks, but there are times you may have to do them, so you need to be familiar with them.

While you will need to perform the function of many gifts to a degree, you need to find the dominant gift God has given you and excel in that gift.

The point is that while you will need to perform the function of many gifts to a degree, you need to find the dominant gift God has given you and *excel* in that gift. That's the one in which you want to wrap up your whole life. That's right, put all your eggs in that basket and give it to God. Don't try to be a "super person" and develop all the gifts to perfection. You will never be able to do that. Most people are able to effectively develop two or three gifts at the most. Take your dominant gift and develop it; use it in daily life and ministry. Excel in that gift. That's the one to make your personal ministry.

Did you know that Babe Ruth was once a pitcher? At one point he made the deliberate decision to stop pitching so he could focus on his strength of batting. He took a lot of heat for his decision because some thought he was a good pitcher. He stuck with his decision though because he knew he had the motivation to be a *great* batter.

Often the difference between being good and being great is making adjustments that allow you to spend more of your time developing your greatest strengths.

Have you ever had an annual performance review where the first part was about the wonderful things you did that year, but then the focus quickly shifted to a discussion about shoring up your weaknesses? It's an all-too-common scenario. And it's probably a waste of time.

Here's why: The "fix your weaknesses" school believes that with enough discipline, determination and training, anyone can do anything. Unfortunately, it confuses weaknesses with limitations. Weaknesses reflect a lack of skill (how to do something) or knowledge (what you know). Weaknesses can be overcome by education, training, experience and practice. On the other hand, limitations reflect a lack of motivation (what you do well naturally). These really can't be overcome, because new motivations cannot be acquired. In fact, if a person has low motivation in a particular area, in spelling, for example, there is very little likelihood that he or she will ever be a great speller. The best the person's spelling will be is adequate. Who wants to be just adequate?

125

> *The "fix your weaknesses" school believes that with enough discipline, determination and training, anyone can do anything. Unfortunately, it confuses weaknesses and limitations.*

It's a much better idea to build on your strengths.

If you want to move up from being good to being great, know what your dominant gifts, talents, and motivations are, and build on them. Why? Because you will develop what you do best and enjoy most. These are your strengths, and they are yours for life.

EIGHT STEPS TO DETERMINING
YOUR SPIRITUAL GIFTS

1. *Pray.* Ask God daily to reveal your spiritual gift to you. Make this a matter of prayer until you are sure you understand what your spiritual gift is or what calling God has for your life.

2. *Examine carefully the characteristics of all the spiritual gifts* in Part II of this book. It will help you determine what your gift is as you evaluate how each characteristic relates to you, and to help those in your church do the same.

3. *Take and evaluate the Your Gifts Survey* published by ChurchGrowth.org. It will give you a profile and bar graph showing your strength and weakness in each of the TEAM Gifts.

4. *Seek the help of a more mature Christian* who has been educated on the principles and uses of spiritual gifts. Let me emphasize, a Christian *who has been educated on the principles and uses of spiritual gifts.* A lot of people who are willing to help you with your spiritual gifts have only a superficial awareness of spiritual gifts. They really can't help you because they don't fully understand gifts either.

5. *Focus on the gifts you do have, rather than on the ones you obviously don't have.* After going through this material, you will recognize that you obviously don't have some of these gifts. While you must not forget the necessity of these gifts in fulfilling your normal Christian role, don't seek to make any of them "your" area of personal ministry.

6. *Select three gifts that you might have.* Several people teach that you only have one spiritual gift based on the word "the" in 2 Timothy 1:6 where Paul says, "Flame the gift of God." Another may quote, "Every man hath his proper gift of God," referring to 1 Corinthians 7:7 (KJV). I believe the word "proper" refers to your dominant gift although other gifts are obviously present. On the

other hand, some teach that all Christians have all the gifts but in varying degrees of intensity.

Scripture does not directly support either position of having only one gift or of having all gifts. In 1 Corinthians 12:29, Paul asks, "Are all apostles? Are all prophets? Are all teachers?" The obvious answer to his series of questions is "no." Therefore, no one can possess all the gifts. But, if you want to take sides, take sides with the second position, because chances are you have several gifts that will vary in different degrees and intensity. You might have two or three gifts and one of them is more dominant than the others. A wide variety and combination of characteristics or motives will be evident in you. One teacher calls it your gift mix,[2] but it's really a combination of several spiritual gifts in varying degrees.

7. **Begin functioning on the TEAM.** This is the most important principle in determining your gift. You can study spiritual gifts from now on and you will never confirm your spiritual gift until you get involved. You must start serving God before you can really be sure of your gift. You have to get a ship moving before you can steer it. Be available.

Begin functioning in areas that correlate with the three dominant gifts revealed in your evaluation. Work as a helper. Go to your pastor and explain what you are trying to do. Say, "Pastor, I would like to become involved with a short-term project connected with (whatever area you are trying)." Or, "May I work in the nursery for a month?" Or, "I'd like to direct traffic in the church parking lot for a month." Or "I'd like to teach in the children's department during the week of Vacation Bible School." Or, "I'll help visit during the four Saturdays of the promotion." Or whatever might appeal to you.

It is especially easy to do relief work in different areas during the summer when people are gone on vacations. The key, however, is not to obligate yourself permanently. Don't say, "Pastor, I think I have the gift of Teaching. Will you give me a Sunday school class

127

to teach forever?" If you misinterpreted, you will burn yourself out. Move around at first. Explain to the pastor why you want to move around and that you are willing to be a helper. Most pastors will cooperate and help you by introducing you to the leaders in these areas.

As you work in these positions, you will get a feel for whether or not you fit in. When does the hand know it's a hand? When it does the work of a hand. When does a foot know it's a foot? When it is doing what a foot does. And the same is true with you. Get involved in the body; get on the TEAM. This is the only way you will truly discover your spiritual gift.

8. *Look for satisfied desires, results, and recognition.* Some people say, "I have the gift of Teaching. The problem is nobody in my class has the gift of learning." If nobody in your class has the gift of learning then chances are you don't have the gift of Teaching; or at best, you haven't taken the time to develop it. Because everyone who has the gift of Teaching will be able to present material that will create some change in the lives of other people. Watch for some satisfaction about what you are doing. If there is none, it is the wrong job for you.

If you don't enjoy what you are doing, you are not in God's will. Remember that God did not call you to a life of misery. The Christian is not to "grin and bear it." He did not call you to do a life of menial tasks, serving in areas that will never bring you any fulfillment. God wants you to live a fulfilled life and your spiritual gift is the source of joy in your Christian life as you serve Him.

HOW TO BE SUCCESSFUL ON THE TEAM

A woman attended a reception with her husband. People were milling around, talking and getting acquainted. A stranger approached her and asked her name. During the conversation, the stranger asked, "What do you do for a living?" The lady replied, "I am the Chief Operations Officer of a small company." The stranger smiled and asked the type of business she ran. The woman replied, "My home. I am a stay-at-home mom." She considered herself a success because she ran her home properly. Remember, *"It is not what you are that holds you back, but what you think you're not."* I am afraid that many people are successful but think they are not.

What is success? To some, success is reaching a certain level of financial independence. To others, it is becoming relatively famous. Some believe it's power. Still others may believe that winning a certain number of people to Christ or building their church to a certain size is success.

The really successful people are those who have found God's will and are living in it to the best of their abilities. It has been wisely said, "To know God's will is the greatest knowledge, to do God's will is the greatest achievement." Success is being where God places you, and doing what God wants you to do with the gifts He has given you.

SPIRITUAL GIFTS AND THEIR RELATIONSHIP
TO YOUR SECULAR EMPLOYMENT

Spiritual gifts were given for the work of the ministry. In many cases, however, they may complement your "secular employment," your job that you have in order to provide for your family. It is very possible that your spiritual gifts can allow you to perform more efficiently in all areas of your life. Highest performance in every area of life is part of your testimony to God's leadership.

Ephesians 4:1 says, "I therefore the prisoner of the Lord, beseech you that ye walk worthy of the vocation wherewith you are called" (KJV). What is a vocation? Our present terminology would say it's your job, but, not so biblically. Your vocation is your total life's calling. It includes every aspect of your life, including your occupation (your job), your

Success is being where God places you, and doing what God wants you to do with the gifts He has given you.

avocation (your hobby), your family, and your ministry. The problem is most Christians want to treat their vocation like it was their avocation—serving God in their religion on Sundays. Serving God, for the true Christian, is a full-time job taking in every God-given priority. It should never be treated as a hobby.

There was a man who had a large and successful tomato farm. He had several hundred acres of tomatoes and sold them to the large food processing companies. He also was very active in Christian endeavors, especially in Sunday school. In fact, he taught a large class of adults and was well known as a Bible teacher. One day, someone asked him, "How can you find the time to teach and shepherd such a large Sunday school class with all your business affairs and other things to be responsible for?" His reply was, "Sunday school *is* my business. I grow tomatoes to pay the bills." Such should be the attitude of the Christian.

Often, knowing a person's spiritual gifts can help in setting a career path which is both enjoyable and a witness at the same time. For example, the Evangelist may make a good salesperson; the Exhorter may make a good writer of training manuals or an instructor for training purposes; the Administrator may make a good manager or supervisor in certain situations.

The word "abuse" in this area is when your spiritual gift is used in your employment *only* and not in the work of God. Let me illustrate.

130

If I gave one of my staff $100 and said, "Take your wife to dinner and have an evening of enjoyment at my expense," I would expect him to do just that with my gift. If he took the money and bought gas and groceries and went home and watched TV, he misused my gift. However, if he bought $10 worth of gas in order to take his wife out to dinner at a nice restaurant, it was not an abuse of the gift. Buying the gas enabled him to take his wife out to dinner.

Someone might say I shouldn't give gifts with strings attached—go ahead. But don't say it to God, because all of His gifts come with strings attached (see Ephesians 4:12, 1 Peter 4:10).

NEXT STEPS

Believers must do more than learn their spiritual gifts. They must utilize them and develop them. God did not give spiritual gifts as ornaments or fancy names to be pinned on His children so they could tell the world "I am a Teacher," "I am a Server," or "I am an Exhorter." He intended for spiritual gifts to be used in His ministry.

In order to use gifts to the fullest, there must be a continuous development process. For many years I, like many others, taught that there were three phases of spiritual gifts: (1. discover or recognize; (2. develop; and (3. use the gift. Like many others, I was guilty of not telling people *how* to develop, and not showing them *how* to use the gifts they have. Now, I realize that is not the proper procedure.

The proper procedure is (1. discover or recognize; (2. use; and (3. develop. *You can develop a gift only as you use it.* A gift in itself cannot be developed. It is developed through functioning. As believers develop and train for specific areas of ministry, and function within their own spiritual gifts, they develop their gifts. A year cannot be spent developing a spiritual gift before it is utilized, since one gift can manifest itself in many different ministries. As a believer utilizes his or her gift within the framework of a given ministry, he or she expands the capacity, motivation, and characteristics of that gift. As he or she develops the ministry, he or she develops the gift. If it could be placed in equation form, it would be:

DISCOVERY + USE = DEVELOPMENT

For example, people with the gift of exhortation will learn more practical steps and be able to help those they teach as they learn how their area of ministry functions best. They will attend seminars, read books and online articles, listen to podcasts or audio recordings, and take advantage of other educational opportunities concerning that particular area of ministry. By doing so, they will expand their gift of Exhortation so that they can relay the practical aspects of that education to those involved with them in that ministry.

Administrators will use the same process. They will learn new management techniques so they can better function as leaders. Shepherds will learn more spiritual traits from the Bible. Teachers will gain more knowledge and facts, and so on. As each learns their ministry, they learn how to utilize their gifts more effectively.

The whole idea is for God's people to recognize their spiritual gifts and spend the rest of their lives utilizing their gifts in the ministry of *reaching* and *teaching* their generation for God.

FOR PERSONAL REFLECTION

1. What four things must you avoid when finding your place on the Team?

2. What would be the worst abuse concerning your spiritual gift and your secular employment?

3. What is the difference between vocation and avocation?

4. What is your definition of success and how do you plan to reach that point in your own life and ministry?

5. Who are the most successful people you know and why do you feel they are successful?

6. Do you consider yourself successful? Why? What do you need to do to improve?

FOR GROUP DISCUSSION

1. **You are a vital part of** _____ the body.

   Every gift is needed or the _____ will suffer. Ephesians 4:16

   You'll never be accountable for God's calling on _____.

2. **What NOT to do.**

   Avoid the _____ and _____ of gifts.

   Avoid making _____ decisions.

   The expression of the gift is more important than the title of the gift.

   Don't make sporadic decisions.

   Avoid "gift_____."

   Key word is BALANCE. Don't substitute gifts for a Spirit-filled life.

3. **What to do.**

   Learn to perform _____.

   Excel in the area of your _____ gift(s).

4. **How it's done.**

   _____: ask God daily to reveal your gifts to you.

   Study the _____ text.

   Take and evaluate the *Your Gifts* _____.

   Seek the help of _____.

   Focus on the gifts you do have, rather than on the ones you _____ have.

   Select the top _____ from your Survey.

   Be available. Function in these three areas as a helper or an assistant.

   Look for satisfied _____, _____,

   _____, and _____.

Note: Answers for each chapter's "For Group Discussion" questions can be found on pages 183-184

PART 2

ACTIVATING
THE TEAM GIFTS

Understanding the general characteristics, strengths and weaknesses of the TEAM Gifts is important. The chapters in this section explain the characteristics based on 28 years of general observations and research. Part of that research involved studying other authors' writings on spiritual gifts and having discussions with and observing those who believe they have these various gifts. The following explanations and the outlines typify certain gifts in the lives of various individuals who possess those gifts. Some are full-time ministers and others are laypeople.

There is no claim to divine inspiration, nor do the lists come from the Bible. The information is simply intended to serve as a tool to help you determine your own gift and to recognize other gifted individuals.

You would be wise to study these chapters at least twice: once for the purpose of understanding your own gift and again for the purpose of understanding other believers so that you can love them and work with them as a TEAM.

As you read you will recognize people around you who fit the characteristics of each gift. If you read carefully, you probably will find a description of yourself and recognize your dominant spiritual gift whether or not you have completed the *Your Gifts Survey*. You will probably also recognize a description of someone in your church with whom you previously had a misunderstanding or problems.

Other gifts will have certain characteristics which are completely opposite from the characteristics of your gift. In light of this, you need to go through this section and really analyze what it says. As you do so, take a pencil and write at the top of the page the name of a person who fits the description in the chapter. (No one will fit 100% of the characteristics, but all people fit into a generalized category.) After you have done that, ask yourself if you have misjudged the motives and lifestyle of that person because of some of the characteristics which are opposite of those of your own gift.

When we understand our gifts, we can understand, accept, and feel comfortable with ourselves. It is just as important that we understand others in the body of Christ who have gifts differing from our own. The secret of unity and understanding in the local body may rest in understanding gift characteristics. As a result, we will love and accept people *because of*, rather than *in spite of*, those characteristics.

Everyone is different because of the particular spiritual gift he or she possesses. We do not have to remake everyone to fit into our mold. We must accept others and amplify their strengths while we overlook their weaknesses. We also must work to amplify our own strengths while we prayerfully and diligently work to overcome our own weaknesses. (By the way, this is also true within the family. It is easier to understand our mates and other family members when we understand their spiritual gifts and the characteristics of those gifts.)

The following nine chapters provide deeper exploration of each task-oriented gift, and how you can activate your gifts in your church. It is my sincere hope that these descriptions will broaden your knowledge and understanding of the nine TEAM Gifts, better equipping you and your TEAM to do the work of the ministry.

THE EVANGELIST

The Greek word *Euangelistes* means to proclaim glad tidings, a messenger of good. It denotes a preacher or proclaimer of the Gospel.

The Evangelist can either be a preacher who stands before a crowd imploring people to be saved, or perhaps an individual sitting across from someone on a plane or in a living room, encouraging for him or her to accept Christ.

The person with the gift of Evangelism usually is outgoing and personable. He or she has mastered a technique of paying compliments to every stranger and asking lifestyle questions such as: "Where do you work?" "How many children you do have?" "In what part of the country were you raised?" When not talking with people about their soul's relationship with Jesus Christ, the Evangelist is often quiet.

The Evangelist is constantly consumed with the need to confront sinners with the Gospel or encourage other Christians to do the same, by directly telling them to do so or by encouraging them with a recent experience. The Evangelist memorizes Scripture in order not to be caught "flat-footed" while witnessing, and often quotes Scripture in an attempt to influence others through God's Word.

Sometimes the Evangelist turns off other Christians and even lost people because of the "sales pitch" used. Some consider him or her kin to the used car salesperson or vacuum cleaner salesperson. However, much of that perception is because of how others view the Evangelist, rather than as a result of the Evangelist's own motives or desires.

The definition of the Evangelist as found in the Greek is an indication of the ministry of any person who has the gift of Evangelism. The confrontational witness (some prefer the term "soul winner") is not limited by lack of opportunities, but makes opportunities. Some people define the gift of Evangelist as a church-planting gift, but that limits the scope of the gift. That definition may have become popular because of the fact that most church planters have the gift of Evangelism and it fits the task of outreach and saturation evangelism needed to successfully begin a new work. Church growth in any type of church probably has at least one gifted Evangelist involved at the center of outreach, regardless of the church's age or size.

Because of the importance of outreach in the church, God has given two ways to evangelize a lost world. First, He gives every Christian the role of witness. Second, He gives some Christians the gift of Evangelism (approximately 10% – see Chapter 6). It is important to understand the difference between the two.

SPIRITUAL MATURITY IN EVANGELISTS
EQUALS CREDIBILITY IN THEIR WITNESS

Philip is the only person clearly identified as an Evangelist in Scripture (Acts 21:8). He was also one of the first deacons (Acts 6:3-5). As such, he met the qualifications of a deacon (1 Timothy 3:8-12, Titus 1:6-8). Note what kind of man God chose as His Evangelist. He was a man with no *obvious problems* in his life. In addition to winning souls, the Evangelist must live in such a manner that reproach is not brought upon the message.

Most Evangelists will probably influence 30 people to every one who is led to Christ, many times leaving the other 29 for someone else to harvest. But if an Evangelist falls spiritually, the 29 onlookers may fall too. Many aggressive soul winners have done more harm than good for the cause of Christ. For this reason, if for no other, it is important that Christians with the gift of Evangelism receive the proper training to help them become spiritually mature and more effective in evangelism.

Most Evangelists will probably influence 30 people to every one who is led to Christ, many times leaving the other 29 for someone else to harvest.

Many new Christians are almost forced to win souls. Sometimes they are thrust into situations they are not yet equipped to handle. Before accepting full responsibility to be confrontational soul winners, Evangelists need to develop some maturity in the Christian walk. This would prevent young Christians with areas that need correction from hurting their witness before those who do not know their past and have not seen the changes in their lives.

The solution is to pair young Christians in ministry opportunities with seasoned, mature Christians who have the gift of Evangelism. The young Evangelist will learn much about presenting the Gospel by watching the seasoned Evangelist minister to the lost.

136

ABOUT THE EVANGELIST

If you are an Evangelist, *you have the Spirit-given capacity and desire to serve God by communicating with people who are beyond your natural sphere of influence and leading them to the saving knowledge of Jesus Christ.*

> **Witnessing Style of the Evangelist:** "If you were to die today, do you know for sure you will go to heaven?" They will confront you directly with a presentation of the Gospel.

Characteristics: The Evangelist Is ...

1. Outgoing and seldom meets a stranger.
2. Well groomed and neatly dressed.
3. Someone who usually keeps to himself or herself in personal times.
4. Fulfilled working one-on-one or with groups.
5. Active socially, gets along well with others.
6. More lighthearted than depressed.
7. Expressive in speech and communication.
8. Subjective rather than objective in viewing things.
9. Tolerant of people and their weaknesses; sympathetic to sinners.
10. Impulsive at times, and not usually self-disciplined; likely to make decisions based on emotions.
11. Peaceable and agreeable in appearance.
12. Likely to display enthusiasm.
13. Talkative and often interrupts people.
14. Someone who enjoys being the center of attention.

Burdens, Desires, and Strengths: The Evangelist ...

1. Has a consuming passion for unsaved people.
2. Believes salvation is the greatest gift of all.
3. Has a desire to meet lost people.
4. Would rather confront the lost with the Gospel than anything else.
5. Is forgiving.
6. Has a clear understanding of the Gospel message.
7. Usually has a burden to memorize Scripture.
8. Finds great joy in seeing men and women come to Christ.
9. Demonstrates an air of competence.
10. Holds the listener's attention.
11. Remembers people's names and faces.
12. Works hard to become a good listener.

137

Special Needs and Weaknesses: The Evangelist ...

1. *Thinks everybody should be Evangelists.*
2. *May be satisfied to get a decision just to get one.*
3. *May turn people off by pressing for a decision.*
4. *Rarely will admit that Evangelism (as "soul winning") is a gift— usually has another definition for Evangelist.*
5. *Believes strongly in "confrontational evangelism."*
6. *Tends to dominate other people.*
7. *Thinks every message must be an attempt to win the lost. This usually causes the Evangelist to be weaker on teaching other areas of Scripture.*

How the Evangelist Is Misunderstood: Others Think the Evangelist Is ...

1. *Not interested in other church programs.*
2. *Typically pushy.*
3. *Aggressive for his or her own benefit.*
4. *More interested in numbers than people.*
5. *Prone to judge their spirituality by the number of souls they have won.*

How Satan Attacks This Gift

1. *Causes pride in number of converts.*
2. *Causes failure to grow and learn.*
3. *Causes the Evangelist to see people as numbers rather than people with needs.*
4. *Causes discouragement when converts are few or infrequent.*
5. *Causes lack of concern for Bible passages that can't be used as "soul-winning texts."*

Where to Use This Gift

1. *In outreach events and visitation programs.*
2. *In special evangelistic efforts, such as ministry fairs, etc.*
3. *In altar calls or invitations to lead new converts to Christ.*
4. *In church planting.*
5. *In gospel teams.*
6. *In migrant ministry.*
7. *In many public speaking ministries.*

138

10

THE PROPHET

Most people think of a Prophet as someone God uses as a foreteller, such as the Prophets of the Old Testament. Today's New Testament Prophet is a *forthteller,* one who tells or "speaks forth" the mind of God: boldly preaching, speaking, and teaching God's Word.

The Greek word *prophétés* means "a prophet, poet; a person gifted at expositing divine truth." While the Prophet who is called to preach tends to focus on pointing out sin and explaining what is wrong, this gift goes beyond the call to expose other people's sin and teach the truths of God's Word, to actually doing something in daily life to use the gift—to expose injustice and expound the truth, and to lead people to make changes that are biblically based. As the prophet "tells forth" God's Word, knowing what God's Word teaches and expects of us, the prophet also leads others to make a difference in today's society and world.

HOW DO YOU VIEW THE PROPHET?

People will view the Prophet's ministry with an *open* mind or a *closed* mind.

> **Open-minded people** will accept the Prophet's teaching. They may become very uncomfortable sitting under a Prophet's preaching because the truth can hurt, but they are willing to do something about it. The next time the preacher preaches, these people come back listening.

> **Close-minded people** will rebel or reject the Prophet's message. I've seen some people get so mad about what is preached, they become red in the face. These people will never grow as long as they are not willing to listen, learn, and change.

The bluntness of the Prophet's message will stir some people to take action and others to get mad. Prophets may find it difficult to pastor a church for any length of time unless they are able to temper the message with a loving spirit and possibly have the gift of Shepherding as well as Prophecy.

One of the biggest challenges for Prophets is to keep a spirit of love. When Prophets keep tender, loving hearts, they will be blessings to their homes, their churches, and to individual believers, making a real impact on their spirituality. In order to do this, Prophets must always "speak the truth in love" (Ephesians 4:15).

> *When Prophets keep tender, loving hearts, they will be blessings to their homes, their churches, and to individual believers, making a real impact on their spirituality.*

ABOUT THE PROPHET

If you are a Prophet, you have the Spirit-given capacity and desire to serve God by boldly and fearlessly proclaiming God's truth.

You are the person with discernment and have the goal of making people aware of sin in their lives so they will repent. You have the ability to easily spot what is wrong and often have to look to find something right. Your concern over the sinful condition of your loved ones, church family, community drives you to pray, and sometimes weep, over them. Because of this, you take every opportunity to share the message of God's Word.

You are a person with a strong sense of duty who speaks out publicly about wrongdoing in any environment, whether home, church, school or community. You will stand up for what is right as well as speak for those who are wronged.

> **Witnessing style of the Prophet:** "You know you are going to hell, if you don't change your ways. So get on your knees and pray this prayer after me." Prophets want to expose sin so people can confess and repent of it.

Characteristics: The Prophet Is . . .
1. *Not very patient, especially with people and their problems.*
2. *Often disorganized and depends on others to keep him/her on schedule.*
3. *Very discerning.*
4. *Usually much more pleasant when not speaking or preaching.*
5. *Someone with a strong self-image, and is individualistic.*
6. *A person with a strong sense of duty, not caring what others think about what he/she does.*
7. *Very opinionated.*
8. *Likely to be more serious than lighthearted about life.*
9. *One who desires to be alone frequently.*

140

10. *Not usually inhibited, but is usually expressive.*
11. *More interested in his/her own aims and desires than others'.*
12. *More likely to be authoritative, especially about Scripture.*
13. *Dominant, not submissive.*

Burdens, Desires, and Strengths: The Prophet...

1. *Is burdened to expose sin in others.*
2. *Must preach—and wouldn't be content just writing.*
3. *Wants to make all the "softies" in the church stronger.*
4. *Speaks with urgency and presses for rapid decisions.*
5. *Desires to see a world without sin—wants to see revival.*
6. *Wants to stir your conscience.*
7. *Preaches for conviction.*
8. *Enjoys speaking publicly and does it with boldness.*
9. *Is more likely to be hostile than tolerant, especially about sin.*
10. *Is usually a disciplinarian who wants things done right.*
11. *Is able to make quick decisions; is seldom indecisive.*
12. *Is sometimes less discerning than they might think.*
13. *Sees problems where others do not.*
14. *Is idealistic.*
15. *Is able to hold the audience's attention.*

Special Needs and Weaknesses: The Prophet...

1. *Does not like to study—relies on others to do background work. Has a poor memory for details.*
2. *Does not relate well one-on-one and is not concerned about being gracious.*
3. *Over-categorizes. Mostly, sometimes, often, and 80% are words the Prophet replaces with "all."*
4. *Tries to convict rather than letting the Spirit convict.*
5. *Judges others quickly.*
6. *Jumps to conclusions and makes decisions before all the facts are available; does not analyze the details.*
7. *Tends to look at the negative side of things.*
8. *Does not make or follow through with long-range goals and plans.*
9. *Tends to be selfish.*
10. *Uses sarcasm and teasing to get points across; is not tactful.*
11. *Is bossy and impatient; has little tolerance for mistakes; wants things done "my way now."*
12. *Is suspicious by nature and cautious about making friends.*

How the Prophet Is Misunderstood: Others Think the Prophet . . .

1. *Is not understanding.*
2. *Looks at a congregation as all bad.*
3. *Makes some people doubt their salvation.*
4. *Is insensitive and cold and has no love for people.*
5. *Is a poor listener.*
6. *Is too self-disciplined and can't have a good time.*
7. *Receives joy in hurting other people's feelings.*
8. *Is too demanding.*

How Satan Attacks This Gift . . .

1. *Causes lack of compassion.*
2. *Causes pride and self-righteousness over lack of certain sins.*
3. *Causes anger and bitterness.*
4. *Causes lack of forgiveness.*
5. *Causes discouragement because of unrepentant attitude by others.*
6. *Causes Prophet to sometimes fall into the very sins he/she teaches against.*
7. *Causes Prophet to rarely say, "I'm sorry."*
8. *Causes a pessimistic attitude.*

Where to Use This Gift . . .

1. *In revival speaking.*
2. *In pastoring when the Prophet has supporting gifts suitable for pastoring.*
3. *In problem solving for a church with a sin problem.*
4. *In counseling to help point out sin in a person's life.*
5. *In preaching on gospel teams.*
6. *In prison ministry.*
7. *In migrant ministry.*
8. *As a mediator.*
9. *As an advocate for just causes, children, or victims of crimes.*
10. *As an accountability partner.*
11. *In ministry planning, depending on secondary gifts.*

11

THE TEACHER

The Greek word for "teacher" is *didaskalos*, which means master, teacher or doctor. The teacher is one who communicates knowledge, guides, makes known or relays facts.

The Christian with the gift of Teaching is not the person we often think of as a teacher in the Sunday school class. The Teacher is the scholar, the person who learns and teaches with more depth than the average Sunday school teacher. The Teacher usually becomes a Teacher of teachers, having the desire to go to great depths to research a project or topic.

There are two areas for which Teachers live: learning and teaching (or writing, if teaching through the written medium). Teachers would rather gain knowledge than to eat, sleep or do just about anything else.

Teachers must learn to teach in two manners that are contrary to their nature. First, the material must be kept simple so students can understand it. Students normally do not have the hunger for knowledge at the detailed level of a person with the gift of Teaching. Secondly, the lessons must be practical, for the Teacher will love knowledge whether it is in practical form or not. The most effective Teacher is the one who can teach more than average knowledge with more than average simplicity.

Many churches don't even have one teacher, while others may have one or two, depending on their community and church needs. Most Teachers (scholars) are found in full-time Christian vocations. The Teaching gift (in its scholarly sense) involves the lowest number of laypeople. The most common place to find the believer with the gift of Teaching is in a church with a Bible institute program, or in a Christian college.

We need gifted Teachers to handle interpretation problems, deeper theology and to teach those with the other Teaching gifts in a more complete manner. People with the gift of Teaching do not necessarily have to teach the Bible to be a help to the church ministry. Teaching in such areas as education, business, finance or computers, for example, may greatly benefit some churches and schools.

Remember that the scholarly Teacher is only one of four teaching or communication gifts. The other three, the Shepherd, the Prophet, and the Exhorter usually have to rely on resources from the Teacher in order to fulfill their responsibilities in the local church.

The most common problems in connection with the Teaching gift are those created by believers who have desires in other areas and find the Teachers to be dull or too deep for their liking. Teachers tend to be heavy on details and light on application. The blessing is that the Teachers (scholars) can challenge us to learn more rather than being complacent with what knowledge we think we already have.

Most teaching aid books, reference books, and commentaries are written by people who have the gift of Teaching.

ABOUT THE TEACHER

If you are a Teacher, you have the Spirit-given capacity and desire to serve God by making clear the truth of God's Word with accuracy and simplicity. *You are the scholar clarifying and explaining the doctrine and teachings of the Bible.*

Witnessing Style of the Teacher: "To get saved you need to start from the beginning. In the beginning, God created the heavens and the earth ..." Teachers must clarify their position with minute details.

Characteristics: The Teacher ...
1. *Loves God's Word.*
2. *Usually enjoys reading.*
3. *Is not usually an extrovert and may be a little shy of strangers.*
4. *Prefers teaching groups rather than individuals.*
5. *Is creative and imaginative.*
6. *Is usually confident in own ability to accomplish; has accurate self-image.*
7. *Is generally self-disciplined.*
8. *Sometimes is technical; usually methodical.*
9. *Is genius-prone.*
10. *Loves charts, graphs, and lists.*

Burdens, Desires and Strengths: The Teacher ...
1. *Has a great burden to know and teach the whole Bible.*
2. *Relies heavily upon the authority of Scripture.*
3. *Has an organized system to store facts.*

4. *Would sometimes rather just do research, but "must teach" because others would not teach it as well.*

5. *Is upset when a verse is used out of context.*

6. *Will question the knowledge of those who teach him/her.*

7. *Places great importance on education.*

8. *Accumulates knowledge and is analytical.*

9. *Is usually objective in making decisions, based on facts not feelings.*

10. *Enjoys studying for long periods of time—likes it quiet; needs time to think.*

11. *Likes to see things clearly and is always looking for better ways to communicate truth.*

12. *Is enthusiastic when explaining and stimulates others to learn; easily understood when teaching.*

13. *Is always concerned with accuracy, often dwelling on the trivial.*

Special Needs and Weaknesses: The Teacher...

1. *Tends to criticize those who differ in doctrine.*

2. *Puts great emphasis on word usage and pronunciation.*

3. *Tends to measure others' spirituality by the amount of their Bible knowledge.*

4. *Finds other people's material hard to present.*

5. *Finds practical application hard to present.*

6. *Has a small need for relationships with people. Sometimes only needs people as an audience.*

7. *Is more likely to talk than to listen.*

8. *Needs to see a positive response from students.*

9. *May have a narrow field of interest.*

10. *Can easily spend more time studying than actually teaching.*

11. *Usually makes friends cautiously.*

12. *Has little tolerance for mistakes.*

13. *Reads directions only when all else fails.*

How the Teacher Is Misunderstood: Others Think the Teacher...

1. *Is a poor counselor.*

2. *Gives too many details.*

3. *Is more interested in presenting facts than in the students.*

4. *Does not have time for them.*

5. *Is boring.*

How Satan Attacks This Gift

1. *Causes pride and feelings of superiority because of knowledge. This is reinforced when others consider the Teacher a final authority.*

2. *Causes the Teacher to lose sight of people's needs.*

3. *Causes discouragement and disenchantment because of others' lack of interest.*

4. *Causes lack of zeal.*

Where to Use This Gift

1. *As a Teacher of teachers.*
2. *As a writer and developer of curriculum.*
3. *As a Bible college or seminary teacher.*
4. *As a Bible institute teacher in a local church.*
5. *As a missionary-teacher.*
6. *As an online or distant-learner instructor.*
7. *As a researcher for pastors, teachers, committees, and special projects.*

12

THE EXHORTER

The Greek word *Parakaleo* means to admonish, to encourage, to beseech. The Exhorter is a "how to" person. Everything he or she teaches revolves around telling people "how to do it." Although the gift of Exhortation has a different motivation than the gift of Teaching, it is still a *teaching* gift.

Exhorters often make the best counselors, because they are willing to spend time with people and give them practical steps to solve their problems. They also can see the big picture—from problem to solution.

Exhorters are people of practical application, yet are very result oriented. Everything they do must be done on a practical basis. They are not very interested in theology or doctrine, but in the practical aspects of the Scriptures. This practicality comes from a desire to teach people how to solve problems and make the necessary changes to be a more mature Christian. (Of course, they wish to be doctrinally sound, but that is not their main emphasis.) They have a strong belief that God's Word has the answer for every problem.

Exhorters have a step for everything. If you go to them with a problem, they might say, "Do A, B, C, and come back next week for D, E, and F, and then the next week . . ." Exhorters are very simplified people who do not like a lot of details. They just give enough detail to get the job done.

Exhorters often end up teaching seminars for Christian workers, helping them achieve more in their ministries. They also make excellent teachers in Bible colleges or seminaries in the area of practical methodology.

Exhorters are also encouragers. Synonyms for "exhort" include such words as admonish, persuade, instigate, urge and appeal. These words carry a sense of urgency. When Exhorters instruct how to live and how to solve problems or to carry out God's work, they usually also encourage the listeners to "get with it" and put the plan to work.

Another aspect of the gift involves what is commonly called motivation. True motivation comes from within a person, but Exhorters are usually able to trigger that inner motivation through encouragement, excitement, and enthusiasm.

147

Exhorters are usually more interested in the positive than the negative. They seldom use, "Thou shalt not" as a way to get people to act. Instead, they use ideas and methods that make the right way seem better to that person than the wrong way; or they are able to make the right way more exciting and practical. They are the encouragers and cheerleaders of the TEAM.

True motivation comes from within a person, but Exhorters are usually able to trigger that inner motivation through encouragement, excitement, and enthusiasm.

THE EXHORTER'S APPROACH TO TEACHING

Exhorters aim to present material that will enable the Holy Spirit to promote change in the student's life. They believe the responsibility of people with the teaching gifts is to take someone who was lost and help the person to become mature in Christ, beyond just engaging in class participation or meaningful discussions. Many Teachers become bogged down with using these good teaching methods and making them the primary goals for the class.

Exhorters use Scripture as it applies to everyday living, not just Bible stories or Bible facts. Many Teachers are guilty of teaching the Bible as a storybook. People know all about Jonah and the whale, the Garden of Eden, and the dimensions of the ark. When it comes to making life decisions, however, they don't know how to apply their knowledge. Exhorters teach beyond just how to win Bible quizzes on Sunday night—but to equip believers for the "in the trenches" realities of Wednesday morning and Tuesday evening.

New Christians need to have basic practical Christian living taught to them. This is where Exhorters help: by giving practical application to God's Word and helping put the principles into practice. Whereas the Prophet can *challenge* the Christian into living right, an Exhorter can explain how to live right and encourage the person to employ tools for practical, successful living.

ABOUT THE EXHORTER

If you are an Exhorter, you have the Spirit-given capacity and desire to serve God by motivating others to action by urging them to pursue a course of conduct. *You are the "how to" teacher, explaining how to apply God's Word to everyday life.*

Witnessing Style of the Exhorter: "If you get saved and live the Christian life, God will help you cope with the daily problems of this world." Exhorters want to show you that living by God's Word is the gateway to happiness and fulfillment.

Characteristics: The Exhorter ...

1. Is result-oriented.
2. Is comfortable working one-on-one or in groups.
3. Is a very practical person; usually analytical.
4. Is usually a good counselor.
5. Is expressive in a group setting; the group listens when he or she speaks.
6. Is usually impulsive; needs self-discipline.
7. Is more tolerant than hostile toward people; usually sympathetic.
8. Has an accurate self-image.
9. Is serious minded, conservative, logical.
10. Is talkative.
11. Is an orderly person, and likes things done in an orderly fashion.
12. Is enthusiastic; usually cheerful and bubbly.
13. Is a person of charts, graphs, and lists.
14. Is bored with trivia.

Burdens, Desires and Strengths: The Exhorter ...

1. Is able to help others find their problems and solutions.
2. Typically shows interest in practical areas while studying the Scriptures.
3. Is burdened to show how Scripture relates to conduct.
4. Has a desire to unify people by using practical rather than doctrinal issues.
5. Puts great importance on God's will.
6. Has several steps of action to solve every problem.
7. Has the ability to motivate others to action.
8. Uses topical messages, most often, when preaching and teaching.
9. Is objective and makes decisions logically, rather than based solely on feelings.
10. Wants to see everyone reach his or her full potential.
11. Believes the Scripture has the solution to every problem.
12. Is a positive thinker; a strong believer in "a better tomorrow."
13. Prefers the analysis to the task itself.
14. Occasionally needs to be alone where it's quiet in order to think.
15. Is extremely creative.
16. Likes being the center of attention.
17. Outwardly demonstrates competence.

Special Needs and Weaknesses: The Exhorter ...

1. May question the value of deep doctrinal studies.
2. May have difficulty accepting himself/herself because of the need of being an example.
3. May be guilty of using Scripture only to support what he or she is teaching, rather than starting with Scripture.
4. Is upset with impractical teaching.

149

5. *Often interrupts other people because of enthusiasm.*
6. *Enjoys motivating people to do more, do better, and do their best.*

How the Exhorter is Misunderstood: Others think the Exhorter ...

1. *Is not evangelistic.*
2. *Makes everything too simple.*
3. *Takes Scripture out of context just to suit his or her purpose.*
4. *Does not use enough Scripture.*
5. *Puts too much emphasis on edification.*
6. *Is too positive when things look bleak.*

How Satan Attacks This Gift

1. *Causes pride in motivational abilities.*
2. *Causes the Exhorter to lose sight of people because of program emphasis.*
3. *Causes discouragement when results are not evident.*
4. *Causes the Exhorter to encourage others to do the wrong thing because of his or her persuasive abilities.*

Where to Use This Gift

1. *As a "trainer" in areas of leadership or methodology.*
2. *As a counselor, especially in a counseling center.*
3. *As a "church training" teacher.*
4. *As a seminar speaker.*
5. *As an online ministry worker.*
6. *As a teacher of premarital classes or other special interest topics.*
7. *As a counselor in a substance abuse recovery program, rescue mission or other program for the needy.*
8. *As a counselor in a halfway house or runaway ministry.*
9. *As a follow-up with new converts.*
10. *As an encourager to those who are discouraged.*

150

13

THE SHEPHERD

The Greek word for pastor is *poimen*. In Ephesians 4:11, where Paul is listing spiritual gifts, this term is translated "pastor." The word *poimen* is translated pastor only one time in all of Scripture; however, it is used sixteen additional times. The remaining sixteen times are all translated "shepherd." Therefore, we must recognize that although Scripture uses the term pastor in this one instance, we are discussing the *gift* of Shepherding, not the *position* or *office* of the pastor.

Though the pastor must have the gift of Shepherding, *everyone who has the gift of Shepherding does not have the position of pastor.* This gift can be utilized in many positions in the church other than senior pastor. The term shepherd and pastor can be used interchangeably, as you will see throughout this chapter and beyond.

Shepherds lead and feed, guard and protect, and oversee flocks. They coach and lead their TEAMS. The main thing on their "shepherd" minds is the welfare of those in their care—their "sheep." They work under a pastor and are therefore an extension of the pastor and must "oversee" their part of the flock.

The Shepherd is not a "jack of all and master of *none*," but a "jack of all and master of *one*." My experience has been that when this gift is used in the pastorate, the individual probably has another dominant speaking gift besides the gift of Shepherding. Although many are strong Evangelists or Teachers, or even Exhorters, most pastors of large churches have a dominant gift of Administration. While the Shepherd's heartbeat is shepherding the flock God has given, the other dominant gift complements their ministry.

Ephesians 4 suggests that if anyone is given the gift of Shepherding, then he or she must also have the gift of Teaching. If you are sure you do not have a Teaching gift, then you can be sure God has not called you to the pastorate.

A Sunday school teacher or small group leader (man or woman) is a Shepherd the same as the pastor is a Shepherd. Sunday school teachers are really pastoring small churches within a church. Their responsibility is to shepherd the class members. The position demands the gift.

First Corinthians 12:11 says that when God gives gifts, He divides "to every man severally as He will." Severally means according to one's own ability. God gives the gift of Shepherding and puts one in a position where he or she can function according to God-given ability. Some may have the ability to care for ten people, thus utilizing their gift in a capacity such as a Sunday school teacher or small group leader. On the other hand, God may give someone else the ability to care for hundreds; therefore, allowing them to utilize their gift in the position of pastor.

Acts 14:23 ("And when they had ordained them elders in every church") indicates that more than one elder is to be appointed in the church. First Timothy 15:17 ("Let the elders that rule well be counted worthy of double honor, especially them who labor in the word and doctrine") indicates that the elders had different ranks, or junior and senior elders. Who are these junior elders or pastors? *They are Sunday school teachers and group leaders.* When Luke penned Acts 14:23, Sunday school did not exist. If it had existed then, the verse may have read, "And they ordained pastors and Sunday school teachers in every church."

Most women test high in this gift because their natural mothering instincts are similar to the characteristics of Shepherding. Women should take this into consideration when evaluating their gifts survey, and may want to look closely at their second most dominant gift also.

ABOUT THE SHEPHERD

If you are a Shepherd, you have the spirit-given capacity and desire to serve God by overseeing, training, and caring for the needs of a group of Christians.

You are the shepherd who leads and feeds: the coach of the TEAM.

The following characteristics are a mixture of the gift of Shepherding in any capacity and the gift of Shepherding in the capacity of senior pastor.

Witnessing Style of the Shepherd: "I'll pray that God will reveal to you your need for His salvation and I'll be there to help you every step of the way." Shepherds want to share in your salvation and personal growth.

Characteristics: The Shepherd Is ...

1. *Usually patient.*
2. *Usually willing to spend time in prayer for others.*
3. *Usually a "Jack of All and Master of One."*
4. *People-centered; loves people.*
5. *Often authoritative.*
6. *More a leader than a follower.*
7. *Expressive, composed, and sensitive.*
8. *Someone who draws people to himself or herself easily.*
9. *A person with a pleasing personality.*

Burdens, Desires and Strengths: The Shepherd ...

1. *Has a burden to see others learn and grow.*
2. *Is protective of those under his/her care.*
3. *Is burdened to teach the whole Word of God.*
4. *Usually doesn't like to present the same material more than once.*
5. *Is willing to study what is necessary to feed the flock.*
6. *Is more relationship oriented than task oriented.*
7. *Wishes to give direction to those under his/her care.*
8. *Desires to look after the spiritual welfare of others.*
9. *Has a high sense of empathy; is tolerant of people's weaknesses.*
10. *Is able to resolve problems between people, compromising rather than going to either extreme—a peacemaker and diplomat.*
11. *Is sensitive to hurt feelings or problems that cause loss of unity.*
12. *Is sensitive to the overall attitude and spirit of the flock.*
13. *Remembers people's names and faces.*
14. *Is self-sacrificing when it comes to his/her flock.*
15. *Is more concerned with doing for others rather than others doing for him/her.*
16. *Is faithful and devoted to his/her flock, often becoming a workaholic.*
17. *Learns to become an all-purpose person in order to meet needs.*

Special Needs and Weaknesses: The Shepherd ...

1. *Fails to involve other people.*
2. *Becomes too involved by doing it all alone; becomes too independent.*
3. *Doesn't hold people accountable to the rest of the group.*
4. *May lack involvement in evangelistic efforts because of already having as many people as he or she can shepherd.*
5. *May become overly protective of his/her flock.*
6. *Tends to use other people.*

153

How the Shepherd Is Misunderstood: Others think the Shepherd...

1. *Should do all the work.*
2. *Should always be available.*
3. *Knows all the answers.*
4. *Should be at every social function.*
5. *Should do all the evangelism.*

How Satan Attacks This Gift

1. *Causes discouragement because the load gets heavy.*
2. *Causes pride because his/her sheep look up to him/her.*
3. *Causes family problems because of too little time and attention.*
4. *Causes selfishness when "sheep" feed in other pastures.*

Where to Use This Gift

1. *As a Sunday school teacher.*
2. *As a pastor or assistant pastor.*
3. *As a special ministry leader (youth, children, seniors, etc.).*
4. *As a volunteer or paid staff member in a shelter for abused, homeless, or other needy people.*
5. *As a den leader for scout troops.*
6. *As a dormitory leader in a college, orphanage, children's home, etc.*
7. *As a small group leader.*

14

THE MERCY-SHOWER

The Greek word *Ellco* means to feel sympathy with or for others. People with this gift are comforters who enter into the grief or happiness of others, having the ability to show empathy. To show empathy goes beyond sympathy. Sympathy feels *for* others, empathy feels *with* others. Empathizers emotionally go through what the victim goes through. They minister to the sick, the poor, the mentally challenged, the prisoners, the blind, the aged, the homeless, etc. They are willing to deal with people, and minister to these people who have needs that most other people feel very uncomfortable working with.

Mercy-Showers seem to always say the right thing at the right time. They are the ones people call first when they hurt because something bad happens, or when they feel great because of some good thing happening to them. When there is a death, Mercy-Showers are the first to be at the house holding someone's hand or fixing a meal. When there is a promotion on the job or a large amount of money comes in, Mercy-Showers hug and jump up and down with the person.

Mercy-Showers are generally not found teaching Sunday school or leading a group since their personality is one of soft-spoken love. They are not usually leaders since they would hurt too much if they had to scold someone or push to get the job done. People love Mercy-Showers because of all the love they receive from them.

Some people think of Mercy-Showers as being weak or compromisers, but they usually have some strong beliefs and principles. It's just that they do not like to hurt anyone's feelings, so they do not express them very often. Some people also have a tendency to "use" Mercy-Showers since they are so easygoing. When church members visit Aunt Matilda at the nursing home or hospital, they usually spot the Mercy-Showers since that's where they spend much of their time. Mercy-Showers are full of prayer requests at any prayer meeting since they are close to those who are hurting.

155

When do Mercy-Showers best use their gift? In times of sorrow and in times of great joy. People with this gift often use it in conjunction with another gift in an area of service, such as deacon, youth worker or hospital visitation minister. That way they get the contacts they really want, people who need their sympathy and a shoulder to cry on.

Mercy-Showers should probably take a counseling course. Since they are sympathetic, they tend not to bring the necessary changes into a person's life to correct the problems that require the counseling. The other alternative is to develop a list of people to whom they can refer people who need counseling or help. That way, they can offer sympathy and understanding and allow someone else to bring about the necessary changes.

For example, if they were to encounter a person who has a problem because of the presence of known sin, it would be good for Mercy-Showers to find Prophets who can confront the sin or Exhorters who can give steps to solving the problem. The TEAM concept of counseling is to use gifted people where their gift will do the most good.

Amazingly, the highest suicide rate among secular occupations is that of the psychologist—the person with all the answers. The reason is possibly that they attract people with problems. Psychologists tend to be Mercy-Showers by nature. They have a sincere desire to help people and the ability to sympathize and empathize with people, often putting themselves "in the other person's shoes." Sometimes they are dragged down by taking other people's problems home with them. Without the biblical foundation, the counseling often doesn't work, leaving psychologists under heavy burdens and frustration because of their failure to help people.

Mercy-Showers must build some barriers on their feelings and establish strong biblical principles to prevent Satan from using the gift as a stumbling block before the Holy Spirit can use it as a stepping stone.

ABOUT THE MERCY-SHOWER

If you are a Mercy-Shower, you have the Spirit-given capacity and desire to serve God by identifying with and comforting those who are in distress.

You are the person who understands and comforts fellow Christians.

Witnessing Style of the Mercy-Shower: "God loves us so much, surely He does not want anyone to go to Hell." Mercy-Showers will tell you a tear-jerker story that will leave you in such an emotional state, you won't be able to resist responding to the Gospel.

Characteristics: The Mercy-Shower Is ...

1. *Usually soft-spoken, though talkative.*
2. *Outgoing with a low-key, inoffensive personality.*
3. *Able to easily express himself/herself.*
4. *Someone who appears to always be loving.*
5. *Usually good-natured and liked by others.*
6. *A person who talks easily with people and is easy to talk to.*
7. *Responsive to people; is a good listener.*
8. *More subjective than objective; decisions are made on feelings more than fact.*
9. *Peaceable and agreeable; does not overpower others.*
10. *Someone who does not analyze the details.*

Burdens, Desires and Strengths: The Mercy-Shower ...

1. *Has a burden to comfort others.*
2. *Is sympathetic and sensitive.*
3. *Likes to fellowship with other sympathetic people.*
4. *Has a heart of compassion for the poor, the aged, the ill, the underprivileged, etc.*
5. *Is patient, but responds to others' needs quickly.*
6. *Attracts people who are hurting or rejoicing.*
7. *Is non-condemning, not a griper (sometimes can be when with other Mercy-Showers).*
8. *Identifies emotionally and mentally with others.*
9. *Is patient, sincere, responsive, tolerant.*
10. *Can become insecure, withdrawn, and somewhat remote.*
11. *Remembers people's names and faces.*
12. *Is self-sacrificing.*
13. *Likes to think about things for a while before making decisions.*

157

Special Needs and Weaknesses: The Mercy-Shower ...

1. *Makes a poor counselor without additional discipline.*
2. *Resents others who are not as understanding as he/she.*
3. *Is not always logical, and sometimes emotional.*
4. *Lets others use him/her.*
5. *Often has a low self-image.*
6. *Can be indecisive.*
7. *Can become a gossiper, especially around other Mercy-Showers.*
8. *Gets depressed easily.*
9. *Is controlled by circumstances.*
10. *May be pessimistic.*

How the Mercy-Shower is Misunderstood: Others think the Mercy-Shower ...

1. *Is weak.*
2. *Is a compromiser.*
3. *"Takes up" for people.*
4. *Is a "softy."*
5. *Is too emotional; cries too easily.*

How Satan Attacks This Gift

1. *Causes pride because of his/her ability to relate to others.*
2. *Causes disregard for rules and authority.*
3. *Causes lack of discipline because of strong feelings for those who hurt due to disobedience and sin.*
4. *Causes him/her to complain and gripe.*

Where to Use This Gift

1. *As a hospital, nursing home, shut-in worker.*
2. *As a funeral coordinator and visitor.*
3. *As a poverty center worker (if properly disciplined).*
4. *As an usher or greeter, welcome center worker.*
5. *As a media worker for shut-ins.*
6. *As a hospitality person.*
7. *As a telephone center worker.*
8. *As a member of a newcomer TEAM, visiting and telephoning.*
9. *As a nurse.*
10. *As an assistant for the mentally ill, long-term or terminally ill, blind, deaf.*
11. *In migrant ministry, released offender ministry, or other unique ministries.*

158

15

THE SERVER

The Greek word *Diakonia* means to do service. In Acts 6:1 the word is interpreted *ministration*. Our word "deacon" comes from the same Greek word. Actually the gift of Serving is a combination of helps and ministering, two expressions of the same gift. The word "helps" is used in 1 Corinthians 12:28, and "ministering" in Romans 12:7.

People with this gift enjoy manual projects. They are not kings; they do not even want to be kings. They are happy working behind the scenes. They are "king-makers."

Servers are *not* people who believe that since they can do nothing else in the church, they must have the gift of Serving. That attitude would belittle the gift and would be an insult to the person who has the gift of Serving. There are no menial tasks in God's work. It is possible that more people have this gift than any other. Servers paint the walls, pick up the trash, sort the hymnals, clean the baptistery, keep the nursery, bake the cakes, cook the meals, paint the signs, drive the bus, and a million and one other necessary tasks in the church. They can always be found late in the evening doing some seemingly small job like fixing the public address speaker that didn't work last Sunday. They usually do not realize that their love for the Lord shows every time the doors of the church are open, especially if they oiled the now-quiet hinges last week.

Let's examine *helps* and *ministering* one at a time.

Helps: Many new Christians are highly motivated to serve the Lord; most have to backslide to fit into the average congregation. They are gifted, anxious, motivated, able to help with the duties of the church, yet inexperienced. That is why new Christians should become helpers—help in Sunday school or in some other ministry of the church. They should even move around and help in different areas of ministry. As they do, they will start to get a feel for what God has called them to do.

Statistics show that most people who don't get involved in the church's ministry within the first six months will not get involved at all. Yet, six months is hardly enough time to train a new Christian to be a Teacher, Shepherd or Administrator.

Statistics show that most people who don't get involved in the church's ministry within the first six months will not get involved at all.

The best way for new Christians to get involved and trained while discovering and developing their dominant gifts is in the ministry of helps.

Ministering: Many Christians will never leave the gift of Serving because it is their dominant gift. They are always spiritually fulfilled because God gave them this gift and they need not be pushed elsewhere to serve. *Most importantly, the gift of Serving should never be thought of as a lowly or second-rate ministry.*

Tabitha (also known as Dorcas) was a woman in the Bible whom God used as an example of the Server (Acts 9:36-42). She used her talent of sewing in the gift of Serving. She was faithful in helping the widows of the church where she served, and she exercised her gift under the lordship of Christ. Just before Simon Peter arrived for a preaching engagement, Tabitha died. The widows showed Peter the dresses that she had made them. Without her help, they would have had nothing to wear. Peter was so touched by the scene that he raised Tabitha from the dead.

Simon Peter had a gift too. He had been used mightily by God as a preacher, a healer and even to raise Tabitha from the dead. Surely his gifts were more important to God than Tabitha's little gift of Serving . . . but when Simon Peter died, no one raised him from the dead.

160

ABOUT THE SERVER

If you are a Server, you have the Spirit-given capacity and desire to serve God by rendering practical help in both physical and spiritual matters. *You are the person who meets the practical needs of fellow Christians and the church.*

Witnessing Style of the Server: "Is there anything you need help with?" Servers feel they must do something for you. Their witness is to show God's love through serving you.

Characteristics: The Server . . .
1. *Is usually ambitious.*
2. *Does not need to be in the public eye to be fulfilled.*

3. *Enjoys manual projects.*

4. *Is involved in a variety of activities and volunteers for many different jobs.*

5. *Is loyal, sincere, tolerant, faithful, and devoted.*

6. *Is usually easy-going, likable, congenial, inoffensive.*

7. *Usually wants people to like him/her.*

8. *Listens to others without being critical.*

9. *Is usually inhibited publicly, not often expressive.*

10. *Is not dominating—more a follower than a leader.*

11. *Is usually good with mechanical work.*

Burdens, Desires and Strengths: The Server ...

1. *Is burdened with others' needs, quickly responds to the needs.*

2. *Is impressed with the need to respond when exhorted to serve.*

3. *Is usually unable to say "No."*

4. *Will very seldom step in as a leader.*

5. *Likes to meet immediate needs.*

6. *Likes to have a good leader to support.*

7. *Enjoys doing mechanical or hands-on jobs in the church.*

8. *Often has high sense of empathy.*

9. *Is usually very patient.*

10. *Avoids drawing attention to himself/herself.*

11. *Is often considered a workaholic.*

Special Needs and Weaknesses: The Server ...

1. *May emphasize practical needs over spiritual needs.*

2. *Is not as concerned about the completed task as the immediate service; has a tendency not to follow through.*

3. *May underemphasize verbal witnessing.*

4. *May jump to meet needs in the church or in other homes before those of his/her own family.*

5. *Has a low self-esteem.*

6. *Needs to know that his/her efforts are appreciated.*

7. *Will take his/her own time, usually working slowly and deliberately.*

8. *Does not stand out in a crowd.*

9. *Likes challenging tasks.*

10. *Attaches to someone who is doing exciting things and allows that excitement to spill over onto himself/herself.*

11. *Is controlled more by circumstances than principles.*

12. *Is only satisfied when he/she has done more for you than you have done for him/her.*

13. *Avoids long-term responsibilities.*

14. *Is a master of decisive indecision.*

15. *Reads directions when all else fails.*

161

How the Server is Misunderstood: Others think the Server ...

1. Is pushy, doing things without asking leaders.
2. Excludes them.
3. Is impatient and jumps in too fast.
4. Interferes with the Spirit's work.
5. Neglects spiritual needs.

How Satan Attacks This Gift

1. Causes pride because of work he/she has done.
2. Causes feelings of insignificance.
3. Causes lack of burden for people.
4. Causes lack of concern for spiritual growth.
5. Causes lack of quality workmanship due to lack of knowledge or skills.

Where to Use This Gift

1. As person in charge of maintenance and grounds.
2. As a baptismal helper.
3. As a nursery, kitchen or choir helper.
4. As an office worker, errand runner.
5. As an audio or video technician.
6. As a record keeper.
7. As a librarian in church library or media ministry.
8. As a greeter or an usher.
9. As an instrumentalist or choir member in music department.
10. As a stagehand in drama productions.
11. As a photographer.
12. As a helper in special ministries such as migrants, deaf, homeless shelters, etc.
13. As a hospitality worker for newcomers or visitors.

162

16

THE GIVER

The Greek word word *Metadidomi* means to give over, to share, to give to, to impart. The important thing here is not to spiritualize and explain away this gift. Some say that this gift refers to giving of yourself and your time; that it doesn't really mean giving money or material resources. On the contrary, Givers honestly feel that the best way they can give of themselves is to give of their material gain for the work of God. They feel that since God gave them the ability to make money, they should use it to give back to God and His work. Everyone should tithe, but the Giver goes far beyond the tithe.

The Scriptures point out Giving as one of the gifts in Romans 12. The Giver is encouraged to give "in simplicity" (Romans 12:8). Most Christians with the gift of Giving do so without fanfare and public recognition. In fact, Givers usually do not wish for people to know whom they are or how much is given.

Givers have the attitude that tithing is the outward evidence of an inward commitment. Tithing is not giving 10 percent; it's receiving 90 percent. It is a commandment for all Christians. The gift of Giving starts where tithing ends.

Givers would look with disapproval on the person who gives with the wrong motive—giving to get (e.g., trying to intimidate God into returning the monetary gift). They would not encourage giving up grocery money, but would agree with giving the money that was saved toward a new flatscreen TV, for more urgent, worthy or eternal purposes. Their motive for giving is always to further the work of God and not to "show off," though some might think otherwise of them.

In Acts 4:34–5:10, there is a significant description of people who had unusual opportunities to give. In the early church, Christian landowners often sold their property and other possessions and gave the proceeds to the church in order to care for those in need. One of those men was Barnabas. He sold his land and laid the money at the Apostles' feet (Acts 4:36-37).

But Ananias and Sapphira sold their land and schemed to give only part of the money to the Lord's work. They lied and tried to deceive the apostles (Acts 5:1-10).

It is interesting to compare the attitudes and the rewards those attitudes received. Barnabas eventually accompanied the Apostle Paul in much of his ministry. God killed Ananias and Sapphira on the spot as a result of their treachery.

The proper attitude about the gift of Giving is probably best illustrated by the story of the Honorable Alpheus Hardy, who used money to support missionaries and educate ministers. His monetary support helped lay the foundations for Christianity in Japan.

During college, Hardy's health broke and he discovered he could not become a minister. "My distress was so great I threw myself flat on the floor," he said of one morning's depression. "'I cannot be God's minister' kept rolling in my mind. It was the voiceless cry of my soul."

During that ordeal God revealed to Hardy that he could serve God with similar devotion in business. To make money for God might be his special calling and gift. The answer was so clear and joyous he exclaimed aloud, "O God, I can be Thy minister." Making money and giving it to God became his ministry.

Another example of how a man's gift of Giving can be so greatly used is Dr. Oswald J. Smith, writer of the song "Then Jesus Came." His desire was to become a missionary. Instead, God placed him in the pastorate and used him to send missionaries and money for missions all over the world. He is recognized as one of the greatest missionary benefactors of recent history.

There must be a distinction made between the *gift* of Giving and the *grace* of giving. First, realize that tithing and giving are responsibilities of every Christian. The tithe is the first fruits of our increase. It is God's and we should give it to Him immediately. Luke 6:38 is for every Christian, not just those with the gift of Giving. That is the grace of giving—giving from a heart of love, allowing God to furnish the returns when we have given from a desire to help others and further His work.

An evangelist visited a college campus where I was attending for a week of meetings. His messages on giving inspired personal testimonies from students who gave and received throughout the week. Many caught the spirit and gave and gave. The problem, though, didn't surface until several weeks later when the students' bills came due. They couldn't pay their bills; they had given the money away. What went wrong? After all, the Scripture does say to give and you will receive.

First of all, the evangelist was not aware of the gift of Giving. He failed to tell us (or was unaware) that all the people in the many overwhelming testimonies had the gift of Giving. When it comes to giving and receiving, some principles apply only to those with the gift of Giving (such as the ability to give beyond their means).

Secondly, some of the students did not have their hearts in the right place. They were not giving to help God as much as to help themselves. *Motive* is the key to giving and receiving. The proper motive is giving to receive in order to give again. These young people were giving to receive so they would have more at the end.

Many Christians, in sheer desperation, have given all they had trying to bale themselves out of a jam, only to see their efforts fail. You can't *give* yourself out of a financial jam, nor can you *give* your way to prosperity with that end as a motive. It's like borrowing to get out of debt.

Givers must observe four guidelines:

1. Do not love riches.
2. Give for the right reason.
3. Make giving your reason for gaining wealth.
4. Keep your spiritual life strong and consistent with God.

ABOUT THE GIVER

If you are a Giver, you have the Spirit-given capacity and desire to serve God by giving of your material resources, far beyond the tithe, to further the work of God. *You are the person who meets the financial needs of fellow Christians and church members.*

165

> **Witnessing Style of the Giver:** "Are there any needs in your life that I can supply?" Givers feel they must buy you something before they can even witness to you.

Characteristics: The Giver . . .
1. *Is usually well organized.*
2. *Keeps to himself/herself.*
3. *Wants his/her gifts to be private, not publicized.*
4. *Usually has the ability to make money as well, but not always.*
5. *Has an accurate self-image.*
6. *Is more likely to be lighthearted than depressed.*
7. *Is particularly interested in helping people.*
8. *Wants people to like him/her.*
9. *Is conscientious and self-disciplined.*

Burdens, Desires and Strengths: The Giver . . .
1. *Is sensitive to the financial and material needs of others.*
2. *Is alert to needs others might overlook.*
3. *Is always ready to give.*
4. *Wants his/her gift to be of high quality.*

5. *Has the ability to make quick decisions concerning finances.*
6. *Wants to know his/her gift is being used properly.*
7. *Usually has a burden for missions.*
8. *Is not the first to give to a project, but will wait for the project to prove itself.*
9. *Is sympathetic.*

Special Needs and Weaknesses: The Giver ...

1. *May measure others' spirituality by the amount of their giving.*
2. *May judge others' success by the amount of their material assets.*
3. *Thinks God has called everyone to give as he/she does, and cannot understand why they ignore the calling.*
4. *Usually gives to projects, but not to individuals.*

How the Giver Is Misunderstood: Others think the Giver ...

1. *Is trying to control them with his/her money.*
2. *Condemns them because they don't give as he/she does.*
3. *Condemns them because they don't have as much as he/she does.*
4. *Is materialistic because of his/her emphasis on money.*
5. *Tries to buy positions in the church.*

How Satan Attacks This Gift

1. *Causes pride because of the amount of his/her gift.*
2. *Causes blindness to spiritual needs and qualities.*
3. *Causes blindness to other areas of service.*
4. *Causes discontent when decisions are made contrary to his/her interests.*
5. *Causes a critical attitude toward those unable to give.*
6. *Causes wrong motives for giving or serving Christ.*
7. *Causes him/her to mistake a burden for giving to missions as a call to the mission field ministry.*

Where to Use This Gift

1. *Anywhere large or small amounts of money are needed to support the Body of Christ.*
2. *As a member of finance or budget committee.*
3. *As a member of missions committee, building committee.*
4. *As a trustee.*
5. *As a member of a school board or commission.*
6. *As a part of poverty, rescue mission, migrant mission committee member.*
7. *As a sponsor to underwrite special projects, radio, TV ministries.*
8. *To meet needs of individual Christians and non-Christians apart from programs.*

17

THE ADMINISTRATOR

A *kubernesis* (in the Greek) was a steersman for a ship. He had the responsibility of bringing a ship into the harbor—through the rocks and shoals under all types of pressures.

Charles Swindoll says, "A *kubernesis* was an expert in the midst of a storm." This is a good definition for the gift of Administration. Leading, ruling, organizing, governing, and administering are words that come from different translations of the Scriptures of the same Greek word. Administrators are Leaders.

Administrators are "take charge" people who jump in and start giving orders when no one is in charge (sometimes when someone else is in charge). They put a plan on paper and start delegating responsibility. The committee or group reports back to them and they work the whole scheme of the program together.

If a program or event is scheduled, they almost instantly have a plan to carry it out. When followed, the plan usually makes the event more effective.

Administrators usually have one of two leadership styles. One organizes things, events or programs. The other organizes people and emphasizes personal relationships and leadership responsibilities.

Perhaps the Administrator is chairperson of the board or the deacons. In fact, without such a chairperson, the board will not function at its best. Some people think Administrators take on too much. Sometimes they have to watch that they do not overstep their authority and expect the pastor or others in leadership to follow them. On the surface they are extremely organized. If they organize things or events, they will usually organize details and have people carry them out. If they are prone to organizing people, they are not detail people, but rely on others to take care of the little things.

They do not often admit to mistakes. They usually do not take time to explain to those under them why they are doing things; they just expect the job to get done. Their patience may wear thin when plans are not carried through as they laid them out.

When things in the church become fragmented, Administrators can harmonize the whole program if given a chance. As soon as a task is completed, they are already working on the next event and start giving the directions before others even catch a breath. They lead by saying, "Come on, keep up with me and we'll set the world on fire." Close observation reveals that most pastors of large churches have this gift. Their ability to lead is a major factor causing the churches to become large.

When things in the church become fragmented, Administrators can harmonize the whole program if given a chance.

But what about the small church where most of us worship? Every position in your church that requires leadership is a potential area to practice this gift. Positions include chairperson of the deacons, trustees or another committee; the Sunday school director; small group leader, office manager; and more. All these areas should have people in them who have leadership ability.

It would be much wiser and more effective if churches would place people who have the gift of Administration in positions of leadership. This would work better than using a rotation basis in positions such as deacon chairperson or trustee chairperson. The rotation system may seem to keep one person from becoming a dictator or getting too much control. However, such a system often causes a gap in progress if someone without the gift of Administration is in leadership for a year or more.

The answer is to retain people who are leaders in leadership positions, holding them accountable using the Scriptures and by providing adequate and ongoing training. They need to learn 1 Corinthians 11:1, known as the "four aces of leadership" verse (i.e. the four "1s" [aces] in the verse number): "Follow my example, as I follow the example of Christ." When one of God's leaders gets a large following, the question is always asked: "Yeah, but are they following God or the person?" They can clearly see that many of these people would not be following God if the person were not present.

The point is that God has always had His leaders. Would the Israelites have left Egypt if they hadn't had Moses, or would they have conquered the Promised Land without Joshua or would they have survived without Esther? God could have chosen a number of ways to lead His people, but He chose the same method for leading as He did for the rest of His work here on earth—*men* and *women*. Throughout history God has always chosen His people for leading: Saul, David, Gideon, Nehemiah, Solomon, Deborah, Esther, and men like Paul. Some were good and some bad.

168

Have you ever read 1 and 2 Chronicles? It can be boring and confusing with all the genealogies and "begats," but, one thing is certain, you will find that all through Israel's history, when godly leadership prevailed, Israel prospered. When ungodly leadership was followed, there was failure.

Even since Bible times, God's leaders have been recognized: people like Martin Luther, John Calvin, John Knox, Charles Finney, John Wesley, George Mueller, Dwight L. Moody, Lottie Moon, John R. Rice, Billy Graham, Jerry Falwell. But from the very beginning, *in the minds of the people,* God's great leaders always stopped with the previous generation. Why is it that a man must be dead before we are willing to follow him, when God has His men and women for every generation, including ours?

ABOUT THE ADMINISTRATOR

If you are an Administrator, you have the Spirit-given capacity and desire to serve God by organizing, administering, promoting, and leading the various affairs of the church. *You are the person who leads the church and its ministries.*

Witnessing Style of the Administrator: "Your life's a mess." Administrators will try to get your life organized before they'll even try to get you saved.

Characteristics: The Administrator...
1. *Is a person with a dream.*
2. *Is goal oriented.*
3. *Is well-disciplined.*
4. *Usually works best under heavy pressure.*
5. *Is not a procrastinator.*
6. *Is often a good motivator.*
7. *Is serious minded, highly motivated, and intense.*
8. *Has an accurate self-image.*
9. *Is more interested in the welfare of the group than his/her own desires.*
10. *Is a perfectionist who wants what he/she is involved in to be done well.*
11. *Loves drafts, charts, and lists.*
12. *Wants things done his/her way now.*
13. *Is prone to being a workaholic.*
14. *Keeps his/her emotions hidden.*

15. Is bored with the trivial.

16. Is dominant, not passive.

17. Likes to be center-stage with people looking at him/her.

Burdens, Desires and Strengths: The Administrator . . .

1. Dreams big dreams for God.

2. Has a burden to move on to a new task as soon as one is completed, usually having already planned it.

3. Delegates wherever possible, but knows when not to.

4. Can't bear defeat—strong desire to win.

5. Can harmonize the various affairs of the church.

6. Is willing to attempt impossible tasks.

7. Is capable of making quick decisions and sticking to them.

8. Will assume leadership when there is no leadership in the group.

9. Is skilled in planning.

10. Makes decisions logically, strictly on facts, not feelings.

11. Is more composed than nervous.

12. Is competitive by nature.

13. Likes challenging tasks.

14. Is enthusiastic, gets people excited.

15. Plans ahead and works on a schedule.

16. Demonstrates competence.

17. Sees the whole picture quickly.

Special Needs and Weaknesses: The Administrator . . .

1. Appears on the outside to be organized, but usually isn't.

2. Looks at the overall picture and may miss the smaller details.

3. May make decisions based on logic rather than Scripture.

4. Doesn't like to admit to making a mistake or to weaknesses.

5. May be insensitive to "little" people.

6. Is often hard to please: his/her standards are too high; he/she is not tolerant of mistakes.

7. Is not good at remembering names.

8. May not be gracious when hurried or busy.

9. Will manipulate others into doing what he/she wants done—uses people.

How the Administrator Is Misunderstood: Others think the Administrator . . .

1. Is cold.

2. Is pushy.

3. Is using them because of his/her lack of explanation.

4. Is not concerned with people.

5. Does not have time for others.

6. Is selfish, trying to be a big shot.

7. *Is lazy if he/she administrates without getting involved.*
8. *Is bossy and impatient.*
9. *Is too independent.*

How Satan Attacks This Gift

1. *Causes pride because of leadership role.*
2. *Causes selfishness because of success; not sharing glory with those under him/her.*
3. *Causes blame-shifting when things go wrong.*
4. *Causes discouragement and frustration when goals aren't met or things go too slow.*
5. *Causes anger and mistreatment of those who disagree with plans, goals and methods.*
6. *Causes wrong motives.*
7. *Causes lack of concern for people or their needs.*
8. *Causes lack of spiritual growth and qualities.*

Where to Use This Gift

1. *As the leader of a project, ministry or program.*
2. *As chairperson of any committee or board.*
3. *As church planner or coordinator.*
4. *As pastor or assistant pastor, business manager.*
5. *As an office manager or department head for large staffs.*
6. *As a Sunday school superintendent, deacon chairperson.*
7. *As the chairperson of building or fundraising projects.*
8. *As the nursery coordinator.*
9. *As a leader of men's or women's fellowship.*
10. *As the head of the library.*
11. *As a camp director or transportation director.*
12. *As director of Vacation Bible School or KidsGames.*
13. *As a women's missionary circle or fellowship leader.*
14. *As the church moderator.*

YOUR GIFTS
SPIRITUAL GIFTS
SURVEY

Your Gifts Spiritual Gifts Survey will help you identify your God-given spiritual gifts. While we recognize there may be other valid gifts today, and many groups have differing views of which gifts are still used today, these nine gifts are the team or task-oriented gifts for use in daily life and ministry. We hope you've decided to take the survey and discover your spiritual gifts prior to reading the book.

If so, that's great. As well, we want you to know that there are three easy ways for you to take the *Your Gifts* Spiritual Gifts Survey and to discover your spiritual gifts:

1. Take the survey on the following pages in this book

2. Take the survey FREE online at TeamMinistry.com

3. Purchase the *Your Gifts* self-scoring Survey for adults, teens or children. See pages 190-191 for more information. *Your Gifts* Spiritual Gifts Surveys are available wherever Christian books are sold and at special prices for group (or large quantity) purchases.

Through this analysis, you will find out in which areas you are "less" gifted and will also discover your dominant task-oriented gift (or gifts). You can then further develop your dominant gift as you exercise it in daily life and in your local church ministry. You will then begin to experience maximum fulfillment in allowing God to work through your unique giftedness.

STEP#1: See the YOUR GIFTS SURVEY questions that begin directly below. Read each statement on the survey and decide how it pertains to you. Then to the right of the statement, fill in the appropriate circle with the most accurate number (0-2):

② **ALMOST ALWAYS** *if the statement fits you 70-100% of the time;*

① **OCCASIONALLY** *if the statement fits you 40-70% of the time;*

⓪ **NOT VERY OFTEN** *if the statement fits you less than 40% of the time.*

Most of the statements deal with your feelings or desires, so be sure to give your own opinion of yourself. Let your responses reflect how you feel at the present time. Remember, there are no right or wrong answers. Do not leave any survey statements unanswered.

When you have responded to all the statements, turn to the scoring sheet on page 181, immediately following the Survey, and follow the directions for adding up your scores.

174

YOUR GIFTS SURVEY

② *Almost Always* ① *Occasionally* ⓪ *Not Very Often*

1.	I have a consuming passion (strong desire, great concern) to reach people who don't know Christ.	② ① ⓪
2.	I put great importance (high priority) on repentance (sorrow, regret, resulting in turning from sin).	② ① ⓪
3.	I believe I am very discerning (perceptive) of other people's motives.	② ① ⓪
4.	When I speak, I desire to stir other people's consciences (make them think, convict them to act).	② ① ⓪
5.	I have an unusually strong desire to study God's Word.	② ① ⓪
6.	I place great importance (value) on education.	② ① ⓪
7.	When I do something, I like to see tangible results for my efforts, such as a finished project or measurable progress.	② ① ⓪

② *Almost Always* ① *Occasionally* ⓪ *Not Very Often*

8.	If I were to teach a group, I would prefer to deal with topics rather than verse-by-verse studies.	② ① ⓪
9.	I am willing to assume long-term personal responsibility for the spiritual welfare of a group of believers.	② ① ⓪
10.	I am people-centered; I need many relationships.	② ① ⓪
11.	I am usually soft-spoken.	② ① ⓪
12.	I am patient, not one to jump into things, but am willing to respond to others' needs quickly.	② ① ⓪
13.	I am fulfilled by performing routine tasks in the church for God's glory.	② ① ⓪
14.	I am usually involved in or drawn to a variety of activities that help other people.	② ① ⓪
15.	I keep my personal and business affairs well organized.	② ① ⓪
16.	I have a burden (heartfelt desire, passion, great concern) to support missions.	② ① ⓪
17.	I make decisions based strictly on facts and data.	② ① ⓪
18.	I can clearly communicate goals in a way that others can fulfill them.	② ① ⓪
19.	I believe salvation is the greatest gift of all, and am driven to tell others about this gift.	② ① ⓪
20.	Some people think my witnessing methods are pushy.	② ① ⓪
21.	I can spot (discern, point out, recognize) sin when other people cannot.	② ① ⓪
22.	I have a desire to tell people about their sin.	② ① ⓪
23.	I like to use visuals and books to support me when I teach or speak to a group of people.	② ① ⓪
24.	I constantly search for better ways to do and say things.	② ① ⓪
25.	I believe I am a very practical, pragmatic person.	② ① ⓪
26.	I am able to provide helpful solutions and advice to others when they have personal problems.	② ① ⓪
27.	I spend a great amount of time praying for other people.	② ① ⓪
28.	I enjoy looking after the spiritual welfare of others; I am protective.	② ① ⓪
29.	I find it easy to express my feelings to others.	② ① ⓪

30.	I have a real burden (heartfelt desire, passion) to comfort others.	② ① ⓪
30.	I am more fulfilled when I work behind the scenes, out of the public eye.	② ① ⓪
31.	I am burdened (greatly concerned) with the physical and tangible needs of others.	② ① ⓪
32.	My giving is a private matter between God and me.	② ① ⓪
33..	I am sensitive to other people's financial and material needs.	② ① ⓪
34.	I am goal-oriented, as opposed to being people- or content-oriented.	② ① ⓪
36.	I work best in a fast-paced environment, under pressure.	② ① ⓪
37.	I have a desire to meet people who don't know Christ, even when they are total strangers, so I can share the Gospel with them.	② ① ⓪
38.	I would rather witness (verbally share the Gospel, give my testimony) than do anything else.	② ① ⓪
39.	I am grieved (bothered, troubled, disturbed, upset) with the wrong actions of others.	② ① ⓪
40.	I am disorganized and must depend on others to keep me on schedule.	② ① ⓪
41.	I have an organized system to store facts and figures.	② ① ⓪
42.	I put more emphasis on the content of material than on people or the task.	② ① ⓪
43.	I am more interested in studying the practical areas of Scripture that I can immediately apply to my life.	② ① ⓪
44.	I put great importance on God's will.	② ① ⓪
45.	I have a burden (compelling desire) to see others learn and grow.	② ① ⓪
46.	I am more relationship-oriented than task-oriented.	② ① ⓪
47.	I am very sympathetic and sensitive of others. I can "put myself in their shoes."	② ① ⓪
48.	Other people think I am weak—a pushover—because of my lack of firmness.	② ① ⓪

② *Almost Always* ① *Occasionally* ⓪ *Not Very Often*

49.	I enjoy working with my hands.	② ① ⓪
50.	I often let people talk me into doing things I do not want to do.	② ① ⓪
51.	I am always ready and willing to give if a valid (real, proven) need exists.	② ① ⓪
52.	I have the ability to quickly make wise decisions concerning finances.	② ① ⓪
53.	I do things promptly; I make decisions quickly.	② ① ⓪
54.	I dream big dreams and have great hopes, although I do not always share them with others.	② ① ⓪
55.	I have a clear understanding of the Gospel and can relate it easily so others understand it.	② ① ⓪
56.	I am socially active and always get along well with others.	② ① ⓪
57.	I must verbalize (speak) my message; I would never be content to only write it.	② ① ⓪
58.	I always express urgency and want others to make quick decisions.	② ① ⓪
59.	Sometimes I would rather just write, but feel that I "must teach" because others would not present my message correctly.	② ① ⓪
60.	The use of a verse out of context upsets me.	② ① ⓪
61.	I develop several steps of action to solve every problem.	② ① ⓪
62.	I question the value of deep doctrinal and theological studies.	② ① ⓪
63.	I am very protective of people under my care.	② ① ⓪
64.	Teaching the same material over and over would be boring and unappealing to me.	② ① ⓪
65.	I attempt to show love and concern in all I do.	② ① ⓪
66.	I act on emotions rather than just logic.	② ① ⓪
67.	I am impressed and motivated when exhorted (encouraged) to serve.	② ① ⓪
68.	I like to meet needs immediately (quickly).	② ① ⓪
69.	When giving, I always like my gift to be high quality.	② ① ⓪

177

70.	Other people misunderstand and think I am materialistic because of the importance I place on money. Much good can be accomplished through using money wisely.	② ① ⓪
71.	I delegate whenever and wherever possible, but I know when and where I cannot.	② ① ⓪
72.	I am willing to attempt impossible tasks for God.	② ① ⓪
73.	I greatly rejoice in seeing people come to Christ.	② ① ⓪
74.	I believe leading people to Christ (presenting the Gospel to non-Christians) is the greatest responsibility given to every Christian.	② ① ⓪
75.	I enjoy speaking in public, and do it with boldness.	② ① ⓪
76.	I am burdened (have a strong desire/conviction, am moved) to memorize Scripture.	② ① ⓪
77.	I tend to question the knowledge of those who teach me.	② ① ⓪
78.	Others accuse me of giving too many details.	② ① ⓪
79.	I have the ability to motivate others.	② ① ⓪
80.	Impractical teaching upsets and frustrates me.	② ① ⓪
81.	I desire to give direction (guidance, instruction) to those under my care.	② ① ⓪
82.	I am willing to study whatever is necessary in order to feed (nurture, guide) those for whom I care.	② ① ⓪
83.	My heart goes out to the poor, the aged, the ill, the underprivileged, etc.	② ① ⓪
84.	People who are hurting or excited seem to want to share their feelings with me.	② ① ⓪
85.	I am already helping people while others are just talking about what to do.	② ① ⓪
86.	I am quick to recognize and respond when other people need help.	② ① ⓪
87.	I want to know my financial gift is being used properly; I believe in accountability.	② ① ⓪
88.	I tend to judge others' success by the amount of their material assets.	② ① ⓪
89.	I want to be a winner; I cannot bear defeat.	② ① ⓪

178

#		
90.	I am capable of making quick decisions and sticking to them.	② ① ⓪
91.	When I share the Gospel or present my testimony to a non-Christian I always press for a decision.	② ① ⓪
92.	Others think I am more interested in the number of people led to the Lord than in people themselves.	② ① ⓪
93.	You must "prove" me wrong before I will go along with you.	② ① ⓪
94.	Studying is too time-consuming; I rely on others to do my background work for me.	② ① ⓪
95.	I prefer to develop my own material for teaching; other teachers' material would be hard to present.	② ① ⓪
96.	I place great emphasis on word pronunciation.	② ① ⓪
97.	Other people think I am not evangelistic because of my emphasis (focus) on personal growth.	② ① ⓪
98.	I am accused of not using enough Scripture when teaching.	② ① ⓪
99.	I enjoy doing a wide variety of activities rather than being confined to only one.	② ① ⓪
100.	I perceive myself as a shepherd (an overseer, guiding and ministering to those under my care).	② ① ⓪
101.	I am an emotional person; I tend to show my feelings and cry easily.	② ① ⓪
102.	I identify emotionally and mentally with others. I am able to empathize (feel with others rather than just for others).	② ① ⓪
103.	Some people think I neglect spiritual needs because of my focus on physical and practical needs.	② ① ⓪
104.	I enjoy routine or hands-on jobs in the church.	② ① ⓪
105.	I believe strongly that people should give financially according to their ability, and I tend to measure their spiritual growth on whether or not they do.	② ① ⓪
106.	I am able to designate large sums of money for specific causes, and am not overly concerned even if others think I am trying to control ministry projects through my giving.	② ① ⓪
107.	When there is no leadership in a group, I will assume it.	② ① ⓪
108.	I have the ability to organize and harmonize the people with whom I work.	② ① ⓪

STEP#2: On the opposite page, transfer your score for each of the 108 statements (i.e., 2, 1, or 0) into the empty box next to each corresponding survey statement. Starting with the Evangelist, on the first two rows on the Answer Sheet (which form bar A), add together the numbers to determine your subtotals from each line. Then add the two subtotals together to determine your grand total for that particular gift. Do the same with each of the following gifts (bars B through I), placing the score for that gift in its respective Grand Total box.

Remember, this is a survey showing your relative strengths in each of God's gifted areas. Its purpose is to offer you guidance as you actively serve in your local church, home and community— which is the only true way to determine your spiritual gift(s). The higher scores suggest your dominant gifts.

After you have discovered your dominant spiritual gift(s), turn to "How to Use This Book" on page 7, to understand how you can use your spiritual gifts to discover God's unique design for you.

NOTE: Additional copies of the *Your Gifts* Spiritual Gifts Survey, (including the 16-page survey, gift summary and answer sheet) are available for purchase wherever Christian books are sold.

YOUR GIFTS SURVEY ANSWER SHEET

A. STATEMENTS — GIFT: **EVANGELISM**

| 1 | (?) | 19 | (?) | 37 | (?) | 55 | (?) | 73 | (?) | 91 | (?) | SUBTOTAL | TOTAL |
| 2 | (?) | 20 | (?) | 38 | (?) | 56 | (?) | 74 | (?) | 92 | (?) | SUBTOTAL | |

B. STATEMENTS — GIFT: **PROPHECY**

| 3 | (?) | 21 | (?) | 39 | (?) | 57 | (?) | 75 | (?) | 93 | (?) | SUBTOTAL | TOTAL |
| 4 | (?) | 22 | (?) | 40 | (?) | 58 | (?) | 76 | (?) | 94 | (?) | SUBTOTAL | |

C. STATEMENTS — GIFT: **TEACHING**

| 5 | (?) | 23 | (?) | 41 | (?) | 59 | (?) | 77 | (?) | 95 | (?) | SUBTOTAL | TOTAL |
| 6 | (?) | 24 | (?) | 42 | (?) | 60 | (?) | 78 | (?) | 96 | (?) | SUBTOTAL | |

D. STATEMENTS — GIFT: **EXHORTATION**

| 7 | (?) | 25 | (?) | 43 | (?) | 61 | (?) | 79 | (?) | 97 | (?) | SUBTOTAL | TOTAL |
| 8 | (?) | 26 | (?) | 44 | (?) | 62 | (?) | 80 | (?) | 98 | (?) | SUBTOTAL | |

E. STATEMENTS — GIFT: **SHEPHERDING**

| 9 | (?) | 27 | (?) | 45 | (?) | 63 | (?) | 81 | (?) | 99 | (?) | SUBTOTAL | TOTAL |
| 10 | (?) | 28 | (?) | 46 | (?) | 64 | (?) | 82 | (?) | 100 | (?) | SUBTOTAL | |

F. STATEMENTS — GIFT: **MERCY-SHOWING**

| 11 | (?) | 29 | (?) | 47 | (?) | 65 | (?) | 83 | (?) | 101 | (?) | SUBTOTAL | TOTAL |
| 12 | (?) | 30 | (?) | 48 | (?) | 66 | (?) | 84 | (?) | 102 | (?) | SUBTOTAL | |

G. STATEMENTS — **SERVING**

| 13 | (?) | 31 | (?) | 49 | (?) | 67 | (?) | 85 | (?) | 103 | (?) | SUBTOTAL | TOTAL |
| 14 | (?) | 32 | (?) | 50 | (?) | 68 | (?) | 86 | (?) | 104 | (?) | SUBTOTAL | |

H. STATEMENTS — GIFT: **GIVING**

| 15 | (?) | 33 | (?) | 51 | (?) | 69 | (?) | 87 | (?) | 105 | (?) | SUBTOTAL | TOTAL |
| 16 | (?) | 34 | (?) | 52 | (?) | 70 | (?) | 88 | (?) | 106 | (?) | SUBTOTAL | |

I. STATEMENTS — GIFT: **ADMINISTRATION**

| 17 | (?) | 35 | (?) | 53 | (?) | 71 | (?) | 89 | (?) | 107 | (?) | SUBTOTAL | TOTAL |
| 18 | (?) | 36 | (?) | 54 | (?) | 72 | (?) | 90 | (?) | 108 | (?) | SUBTOTAL | |

DO YOU WANT TO KNOW CHRIST?

As you reach the end of this book, you may be at a crossroads in your life. For some of you, the thought of knowing Christ as your personal Savior might be a new concept, while for others it might be something you've thought about for a long time. Either way, the good news is that asking Jesus to be your Lord and Savior is not out of reach or far away. If God is pulling at your heart right now, and you feel compelled to give your life to Christ, I invite you to tell Him so in your own words, or pray this simple prayer:

Dear Jesus, I admit that I am a sinner and that I fall far short of Your glory. My sins have caused a wide gulf between eternal life and me, and I know that You are the Way, the Truth, and the Life that bridges that gap and leads me into a relationship with God forever. I accept the grace of Your forgiveness, Jesus, and by faith know that You died on the Cross for my sins, and that through You I may know the Father. Thank You for hearing my prayer, and for Your unconditional love toward me. Now let me walk in Your mercy, and give me the wisdom, strength, and desire to walk with You each day forward. In Christ's name, amen.

If you have just prayed to receive Christ as your Savior, I invite you to tell your Christian friends and family, who can help you in your next steps as a new believer. As well, I urge you to read the Bible, starting with the four Gospels (Matthew, Mark, Luke, John), and find a church that teaches the Bible as God's Word. And congratulations for making the most important decision of your life!

"FOR GROUP DISCUSSION" ANSWERS

Chapter 1 – Eight Reasons Why Every Christian Should Know Their Spiritual Gift

Knowing your spiritual gift . . .

1. . . . helps you understand the Holy Spirit's work through you.
2. . . . helps you know what God has not called you to do.
3. . . . relieves you from serving out of guilt or duty.
4. . . . helps you understand how the Holy Spirit wants to use you.
5. . . . fulfills a deep need to serve God effectively.
6. . . . builds unity among believers.
7. . . . equips you to fulfill God's calling for you life.
8. . . . adds to your self–acceptance.

Chapter 2 – What Is a Spiritual Gift?

1. Spiritual gifts are the building blocks of the church.
2. A spiritual gift is a supernatural capacity.
3. Spiritual gifts are the tools for doing the work of the ministry.
4. A spiritual gift is the source of joy in your Christian life.
5. A spiritual gift is a supernatural desire.
6. A spiritual gift is a divine calling.
7. A spiritual gift divinely influences your motives or reasons for doing things.
8. A spiritual gift is a divine privilege and responsibility.

Chapter 3 - Spiritual Gifts and Their Relationship to God's Will

The will of God for your life is not...

1. bad
2. fixed
3. lost
4. revealed to others
5. based on circumstances
6. contrary to God's Word

God's will for your life is that you be:

1. saved
2. sanctified
3. Spirit-filled
4. submissive
5. suffer
6. serve
7. whatever you desire

Chapter 4 – Spiritual Gifts and Their Relationship to the Believer

1. Every true Christian has at least one spiritual gift. No one has all the spiritual gifts.
2. Every Christian receives at least one spiritual gift as evidenced in Scripture.
3. God determines which spiritual gift you receive.

Do not confuse the spiritual gifts with:

1. The fruit of the Spirit
2. Natural talent.
3. A place of service.
4. An age-specific ministry.
5. A subject-specific ministry.
6. Christian roles or responsibilities.

Gift Classifications

1. Most scholars agree on three classifications of gifts.

   Positions of Miraculous Gifts

   a. Extreme Charismatic
   b. Charismatic
   c. Limited Charismatic
   d. Non-Charismatic
   e. Anti-Charismatic

Two Other Types of Gifts Groups Are . . .

2. Enabling gifts.
3. Team gifts.

Chapter 5 – Team Ministry

1. The human body
2. The body of Christ
3. The church
4. The members
5. The spiritual gifts of those members

The final question asks you to fill in the blank Team Ministry Chart on page 83. The answers for the needs and provisions in this chart can be found on page 67.

Chapter 6 – The Gift of Evangelism and Its Relationship to Evangelism

1. There are only two groups responsible for doing evangelism:

   Group one is Christians with the gift of Evangelism.

   Group two is Christians without the gift of Evangelism.

2. The key to reaching people for Christ is . . . friends and family, or "existing relationships."

3. The method is either confrontational evangelism, lifestyle evangelism, or team evangelism.

4. The dominant philosophy and method of evangelism for the past twenty years is: the Seeker-sensitive model.

   But, the people we really want to reach for Christ are non-Seekers.

5. Seeker-oriented methodology won't work for reaching and influencing non-Seekers in today's culture.

6. We must develop trusting relationships.

7. AMEs are Acquaintance Making Events, or an event for the purpose of introducing non-saved and non-churched friends to other church members.

8. RSAs are Relationship Strengthening Activities, or any activity for the purpose of developing, cultivating, strengthening, and building trusting relationships between your non-churched friends and other church members.

Chapter 7 – Abusing the Gifts

1. Gift Ignorance is a lack of knowledge regarding the possession of spiritual gifts and their function.

2. Gift Blindness results from gift ignorance and renders victims incapable of recognizing their own spiritual gifts and the influence of gifts on their own life and ministry.

3. Gift Imposing is the act of forcing one's spiritual gifts upon another and attempting to compel them to perform as though it were God's gift to them.

4. Gift Gravitation refers to the tendency among Christians to attract and be attracted to other Christians with like spiritual gifts.

5. Gift Colonization is the direct and inescapable result of unrestrained gift gravitation.

6. Gift Coveting is the activity of desiring a gift other than that which has been given to the individual by the Holy Spirit.

Chapter 8 – How to Discover Your Spiritual Gift

1. You are a vital part of the team and the body.

   Every gift is needed or the whole body will suffer.

   You'll never be accountable for God's calling on someone else's life.

2. What NOT to do.

   Avoid the abuses and misuses of gifts.

   Avoid making impulsive decisions.

   Avoid "gift obsession."

3. What to do.

   Learn to perform all the gifts.

   Excel in the area of your dominant gift(s).

4. How it's done.

   Pray: ask God daily to reveal your gifts to you.

   Study the characteristics of all the spiritual gifts within this text.

   Take and evaluate the *Your Gifts* Survey. Seek the help of a more mature Christian who has been educated on the principles and uses of spiritual gifts.

   Focus on the gifts you do have, rather than on the ones you don't have. Select the top three gifts from your Survey.

   Look for satisfied desires, results, and recognition.

Arn, Charles, McGavran, Donald and Arn, Win. *Growth A New Vision for the Sunday School.* Pasadena, CA: Church Growth Press, 1980.

Arn, Win (edited by). *The Pastor's Church Growth Handbook, Volume I.* Pasadena, CA: Church Growth Press, 1979.

(edited by). *The Pastor's Church Growth Handbook, Volume II.* Pasadena, CA: Church Growth Press, 1982.

Arthur, Kay. *How to Discover Your Spiritual Gifts.* Chattanooga, TN: Reach Out, Inc., 1977.

Bennett, Dennis and Rita. *The Holy Spirit and You.* Plainfield, NJ: Logos International, 1971.

Bittlinger, Arnold. *Gifts and Graces.* Grand Rapids, MI: William B. Eerdmans Publishing Company, 1967.

Blanchard, Tim. *A Practical Guide to Finding Your Spiritual Gifts.* Wheaton, IL: Tyndale House Publishers, Inc., 1979.

Bridge, Donald and Phypers, David. *Spiritual Gifts & The Church.* Downers Grove, IL: InterVarsity Press, 1973.

Brown, Woodrow (edited by). *The Person and Work of the Holy Spirit.* Bible School Park, NY: Echoes Publishing Company, 1948. (By senior students of the classes of 1947 and 1948 as taught by Rev. H. H. Wagner, D.D., in the Systematic Theology course at the Practical Bible Training School, Bible School Park, Broome County, NY. Editor Woodrow Brown was President of the class of 1948.)

Bugbee, Bruce, Don Cousins and Bill Hybels, *Network,* Grand Rapids, MI, Zondervan Publishing House, 1994

Bullinger, E. W. *The Giver and His Gifts.* Grand Rapids, MI: Kregel Publications, 1905.

Carter, Howard. *Spiritual Gifts and Their Operation.* Springfield, MO: Gospel Publishing House, 1968.

Charles E. Fuller Institute. *Spiritual Gifts & Church Growth Leaders' Guide,* Pasadena, CA: Charles E. Fuller Institute, 1978.

Christenson, Larry. *Speaking In Tongues.* Minneapolis, MN: Dimension Books, 1968.

The Gift of Tongues. Minneapolis, MN: Bethany Fellowship, Inc., 1963.

Clark, Martin E. *Choosing Your Career: The Christian's Decision Manual.* Phillipsburg, NJ: Presbyterian and Reformed Publishing Company, 1981.

Clark, Steve. *Baptized in the Spirit and Spiritual Gifts.* Pecos, NM: Dove Publications, 1969.

Clayton, Lynn P. *No Second-Class Christians.* Nashville, TN: Broadman Press, 1976.

Clinton, Bobby. *Spiritual Gifts.* Coral Gables, FL: Learning Resource Center Publications, 1975.

Criswell, W. A. *The Baptism, Filling & Gifts of the Holy Spirit.* Grand Rapids, MI: Zondervan Publishing House, 1973.

The Holy Spirit in Today's World. Grand Rapids, MI: Zondervan Publishing House, 1966.

Cumming, James Elder. *A Handbook on The Holy Spirit.* Minneapolis, MN: Dimension Books, 1965.

Dale, Robert D. *To Dream Again.* Nashville, TN: Broadman Press, 1981.

David C. Cook Publishing Co. *Congratulations-You're Gifted.* Elgin, IL: David C. Cook Publications, 1957.

Dillon, William S. *God's Work in God's Way.* Woodworth, WI: Brown Gold Publications, 1957.

Dollar, George W., Ph.D. *The New Testament and New Pentecostalism.* Maple Grove, MN: Nystrom Publishing Company, 1978.

Edwards, Gene. *How to Have a Soul Winning Church.* Springfield, MO: Gospel Publishing House, 1962.

Engstrom, Ted. W. *Your Gift of Administration How to Discover and Use It.* Nashville, TN: Thomas Nelson Publishers, 1979.

Epp, Theodore H. *Spiritual Gifts for Every Believer.* Lincoln, NE: Back to the Bible, 1962.

Falwell, Jerry, Ed Dobson, and Ed Hindson, editors. *The Fundamentalist Phenomenon.* Garden City, NY: Doubleday and Company, Inc., 1981.

Felker, Lenoir M. *The Fruit and Gifts of the Holy Spirit Teacher's Manual.* Marion, IN: The Wesley Press, 1979.

Finney, Charles G. (Compiled and edited by Timothy L. Smith) *The Promise of The Spirit.* Minneapolis, MN: Bethany House Publishers, 1980.

Fisk, Samuel. *Divine Healing Under the Searchlight.* Schaumburg, IL: Regular Baptist Press, 1978.

Flynn, Leslie B. *19 Gifts of The Spirit.* Wheaton, IL: Victor Books, 1974.

Frost, Robert C., Ph.D. *Aglow with The Spirit.* Plainfield, NJ: Logas International, 1965.

Gangel, Kenneth O. *You and Your Spiritual Gifts.* Chicago, IL: Moody Press, 1975.

Unwrap Your Spiritual Gifts. Wheaton, IL: Victor Books, 1983.

Gardiner, George E. *The Corinthian Catastrophe.* Grand Rapids, MI: Kregel Publications, 1974.

Gee, Donald. *Concerning Spiritual Gifts.* Springfield, MO: Gospel Publishing House, 1961.

Spiritual Gifts in the Work of the Ministry Today. Springfield, MO: Gospel Publishing House, 1963.

Toward Pentecostal Unity. Springfield, MO: Gospel Publishing House, 1961.

Gillquist, Peter E. *Let's Quit Fighting About The Holy Spirit.* Grand Rapids, MI: Zondervan Publishing House, 1974.

Gordon, A.J. *The Ministry of The Spirit.* Minneapolis, MN: Bethany Fellowship, Inc., 1964.

Gower, David M. *Questions of the Charismatics.* Schaumburg, IL: Regular Baptist Press, 1981.

Graham, Billy. *The Holy Spirit Activating God's Power In Your Life.* Waco, TX: Word Books, 1978.

Griffiths, Michael. *Grace-Gifts.* Grand Rapids, MI: William B. Eerdmans Publishing Company, 1978.

Hagin, Kenneth E. *Seven Vital Steps to Receiving The Holy Spirit.* Tulsa, OK: Kenneth Hagin Ministries, Inc., 1980.

Concerning Spiritual Gifts. Tulsa, OK: Kenneth Hagin Ministries, Inc., 1974.

Hauck, Gary. L. *Is My Church What God Meant It to Be.* Denver, CO: Accent B/P Publications, 1979.

Hendrix, John D. *Nexus.* Nashville, TN: Convention Press, 1974.

Hickey, Marilyn. *Seven Gifts To Success.* Denver, CO: Life for Laymen, Inc., 1976.

Hocking, David L. *Spiritual Gifts.* Sounds of Grace Ministries, 1975.

Horton, Harold. *The Gifts of The Spirit.* Springfield, MO: Gospel Publishing House, 1934.

Hubbard, David Allan. *Unwrapping The Gifts of God.* Pasadena, CA: Fuller Evangelistic Association, 1983.

Hurn, Raymond, W., Dr. *Finding Your Ministry.* Kansas City, MO: Beacon Hill Press of Kansas City, 1979.

Spiritual Gifts Workshop. Kansas City, MO: Department of Home Missions, 1978.

Hutchins, Clair Dean and Gibson, Brother John. *Winning the World .* St. Petersburg, FL: World Mission Crusade, 1985.

Hutson, Curtis, Dr. *The Fullness of the Holy Spirit.* Murfreesboro, TN: Sword of The Lord Publishers, 1981.

Hyles, Jack, Dr. *Meet The Holy Spirit.* Hammond, IN: Hyles-Anderson Publishers, 1982.

Innes, Dick. *I Hate Witnessing.* Ventura, CA: Vision House, 1983.

Institute For American Church Growth: *How to Mobilize Your Laity for Ministry Through Your Church.* Pasadena, CA: Institute for American Church Growth.

Spiritual Gifts for Building the Body. Pasadena, CA: Institute for American Church Growth, 1979.

Ironside, H. A. *The Mission of The Holy Spirit and Praying in The Holy Spirit.* Neptune, NJ: Loizeaux Brothers, 1957.

Jowett, J. H. *Life in the Heights.* Grand Rapids, MI: Baker Book House, 1925.

Judisch, Douglas. *An Evaluation of Claims to the Charismatic Gifts.* Grand Rapids, MI: Baker Book House, 1978.

Kilinski, Kenneth K. and Wofford, Jerry C. *Organization and Leadership in the Local Church.* Grand Rapids, MI: Zondervan Publishing House, 1973.

Kinghorn, Kenneth Cain. *Gifts of the Spirit.* Nashville, TN: Abingdon Press, 1976.

Discovering Your Spiritual Gifts: A Personal Method. Wilmore, KY: Francis Asbury Publishing Company, Inc., 1981.

Koch, Kurt. *Charismatic Gifts.* Quebec, Canada: The Association for Christian Evangelism (Quebec) Inc., 1975.

The Strife of Tongues. Grand Rapids, MI: Kregel Publications, 1969.

Kuyper, Abraham, D. D., LL.D., (translated from the Dutch with Explanatory Notes by Rev. Henri De Vries). *The Work of The Holy Spirit.* Grand Rapids, MI: Wm. B. Eerdmans Publishing Co., 1900.

LeTourneay, R. G. *Mover of Men and Mountains.* Chicago, IL: Moody Press, 1960.

Lightner, Robert P. *Speaking in Tongues and Divine Healing.* Schaumburg, IL: Regular Baptist Press, 1965.

Lovett, C. S. *Witnessing Made Easy.* Baldwin Park, CA: Personal Christianity, 1964.

MacArthur, John F., Jr. *The Charismatics: A Doctrinal Perspective.* Grand Rapids, MI: Zondervan Publishing House, 1978.

Keys To Spiritual Growth. Old Tappan, NJ: Fleming H. Revell Company, 1976.

MacGorman, J. W. *The Gifts of The Spirit.* Nashville, TN: Broadman Press, 1974.

Martin, Paul. *The Holy Spirit.* Kansas City, MO: Beacon Hill Press of Kansas City, 1970.

Mattson, Ralph and Miller, Arthur. *Finding a Job You Can Love.* Nashville, TN: Thomas Nelson Publishers, 1982.

Maxwell, John C., Dr. *Biblically Teaching Spiritual Gifts.* San Diego, CA:

and Reiland, Dan M. *A Practical Guide to Lay Involvement in Your Church.* Lemon Grove, CA: Skyline Wesleyan Church, 1983.

McGee, J. Vernon. *I Corinthians.* Pasadena, CA: Thru The Bible Books, 1977.

Ephesians. Pasadena, CA: Thru The Bible Books, 1977.

Talking in Tongues! Pasadena, CA: Thru The Bible Books, 1963.

Gifts of The Spirit. Pasadena, CA: Thru The Bible Books, 1979.

McMinn, Gordon N., Ph.D. *Spiritual Gifts Survey.* Portland, OR: Western Baptist Press, 1978.

McNair, Jim. *Experiencing The Holy Spirit.* Minneapolis, MN: Bethany Fellowship, Inc., 1977.

McRae, William J. *The Dynamics of Spiritual Gifts.* Grand Rapids, MI: Zondervan Publishing House, 1976.

McSwain, Jay, *Finding Your PLACE In Ministry.* Oklahoma City, OK; PLACE Ministries, 2000.

Miller, Arthur F. and Mattson, Ralph T. *The Truth About You.* Old Tappan, NJ: Fleming H. Revell Company, 1977.

Miller Basil. *George Muller Man of Faith & Miracles.* Minneapolis, MN: Dimension Books, 1941.

Mundell, George H. *The Ministry of The Holy Spirit.* Darby, PA: Maranatha Publications, date unknown.

Murray, Andrew (edited by). *The Power of The Spirit: Selections from the Writings of William Law.* Minneapolis, MN: Dimension Books, 1977.

Neighbour, Ralph W., Jr. *This Gift is Mine.* Nashville, TN: Broadman Press, 1974.

Nystrom, Carolyn. *The Holy Spirit in Me.* Chicago, IL: Moody Press, 1980.

O'Connor, Elizabeth. *Eighth Day of Creation.* Waco, TX: Word Books, 1971.

Owen, John, D. D. *The Holy Spirit His Gifts and Power.* Grand Rapids, MI: Kregel Publications, 1954.

Pache, Rene (Translated by J. D. Emerson, Vennessur Lausanne). *The Person and Work of The Holy Spirit.* Chicago, IL: Moody Press, 1954.

Palmer, John M. *Equipping for Ministry.* Springfield, MO: Gospel Publishing House, 1985.

Pearlman, Myer. *Let's Meet The Holy Spirit.* Springfield, MO: Gospel Publishing House, 1935.

Picirilli, Robert E. *The Gifts of The Spirit.* Nashville, TN: Randall House Publications, 1980.

Pickering, Ernest, Dr. *Charismatic Confusion.* Schaumburg, IL: Regular Baptist Press, 1976.

Prange, Erwin E. *The Gift Is Already Yours.* Minneapolis, MN: Bethany Fellowship, Inc., 1980.

Purkiser, W. T. *The Gifts of The Spirit.* Kansas City, MO: Beacon Hill Press of Kansas City, 1975.

Rea, Joh, Editor with several contributing editors. *The Layman's Commentary on The Holy Spirit.* Plainfield, NJ: Logos International, 1972.

Reeves, R. Daniel and Jenson, Ronald. *Always Advancing: Modern Strategies for Church Growth.* San Bernardino, CA: Here's Life Publishers, Inc., 1984.

Rice, John R., Dr. *The Charismatic Movement.* Murfreesboro, TN: Sword of The Lord Publishers, 1976.

How Jesus, Our Pattern, Was Filled With The Holy Spirit. Murfreesboro, TN: Sword of The Lord Publishers, 1946.

How Great Soul Winners Were Filled With The Holy Spirit. Murfreesboro, TN: Sword of The Lord Publishers, 1949.

The Fullness of The Spirit. Murfreesboro, TN: Sword of The Lord Publishers, 1946.

The Christian and The Holy Spirit. Murfreesboro. TN: Sword of The Lord Publishers, 1972.

Ridenhour, Lynn. *Spirit Aflame: An Autobiography.* St. Paul, MN: Braun Press, 1980.

Robison, James. *New Growth: What The Holy Spirit Wants to do for You.* Wheaton, IL: Tyndale House, 1978.

Ryrie, Charles Caldwell. *The Holy Spirit.* Chicago, IL: Moody Press, 1965.

Schlink, Basilea. *Ruled by The Spirit.* Minneapolis, MN: Dimension Books, 1969.

Schuller, Robert H. *Self Esteem: The New Reformation.* Waco, TX: Word Books, 1982.

Senter, Mark, III. *The Art of Recruiting Volunteers.* Wheaton, IL: Victor Books, 1960.

Settel, T. S. (edited by). *The Faith of Billy Graham.* New York, NY: The New American Library, Inc., 1968.

Smith, Charles R. *Tongues in Biblical Perspective.* Winona Lake, IN: BMH Books, 1972.

Stanger, F. B. *The Gifts of the Spirit.* Harrisburg, PA: Christian Publications Inc., 1974.

Stedman, Ray C. *Body Life.* Glendale, CA: Regal Books, 1972.

A Study Guide for Body Life. Glendale, CA: Regal Books, 1977.

Swindoll, Charles R. *Tongues: An Answer to Charismatic Confusion.* Portland, OR: Multnomah Press, 1981.

Synan, Vinson, Editor. *Aspects of Pentecostal-Charismatic Origins*. Plainfield, NJ: Logos International, 1975.

Taylor, Jack R. *After The Spirit Comes . . . .* Nashville, TN: Broadman Press, 1974.

The Sunday School Board of the Southern Baptist Convention. *Discovering Your Spiritual Gifts*. Nashville, TN: The Sunday School Board of the Southern Baptist Convention, 1981.

Thomas, Robert, L. *Understanding Spiritual Gifts*. Chicago, IL: Moody Press, 1978.

Torrey, R. A. *The Baptism with the Holy Spirit*. Minneapolis, MN: Dimension Books, 1972.

How to Find Fullness of Power in Christian Life and Service. Minneapolis, MN: Bethany House Publishers, 1903.

Tournier, Paul. *The Meaning of Gifts*. Atlanta, GA: John Knox Press, 1961.

Towns, Elmer. *A Fresh Start in Life Now That You Are a Christian*. Roanoke, VA: Progress Press, Inc., 1976.

What The Faith is All About. Wheaton, IL: Tyndale House Publishers, Inc., 1983.

What The Faith is All About: Leader's Guide. Wheaton, IL: Tyndale House Publishers, Inc., 1984.

Say-It-Faith. Wheaton, IL: Tyndale House Publishers, Inc., 1983.

Tozer, A. W. *Tragedy in the Church: The Missing Gifts*. Harrisburg, PA: Christian Publications, Inc., 1978.

Unger, Merrill, F. *The Baptism & Gifts of the Holy Spirit*. Chicago, IL: Moody Press, 1974.

Van Der Puy, Abe C. *The Holy Calling of God: You Can Serve Successfully*. Lincoln, NE: Back to the Bible, 1982.

Vaughan, C. R., D. D. *The Gifts of The Holy Spirit*. Carlisle, PA: The Banner of Truth Trust, 1894.

Wagner, C. Peter. *Your Spiritual Gifts Can Help Your Church Grow*. Glendale, CA: Regal Books, 1979.

Your Church Can Grow. Glendale, CA: Regal Books, 1976.

Your Church Can Be Healthy. Nashville, TN: Abingdon, 1979.

Walvoord, John F., A. M., Th. D. *The Holy Spirit*. Grand Rapids, MI: Zondervan Publishing House, 1954.

Watts, Wayne. *The Gift of Giving*. Colorado Springs, CO: NavPress, 1982.

Webley, Simon. *How to Give Away Your Money*. Downers Grove, IL: InterVarsity Press, 1978.

Wemp, C. Sumner. *How on Earth Can I Be Spiritual?* Nashville, TN: Thomas Nelson, Inc., Publishers, 1978.

Wesley, John as paraphrased by Clare Weakley. *The Holy Spirit and Power*. Plainfield, NJ: Logos International, 1977.

Williams, John, *The Holy Spirit, Lord and Life-Giver Study Guide*. Neptune, NJ: Loizeaux Brothers, 1980.

The Holy Spirit. Lord and Life-Giver Study Guide. Neptune, NJ: Loizeaux Brothers, 1980.

Willmington, Harold. *The Doctrine of the Holy Spirit*. Lynchburg, VA: personal publication.

Winslow, Octavius. *The Work of The Holy Spirit*. Carlisle, PA: The Banner of Truth Trust, 1840.

Yocum, Bruce. *Prophecy: Exercising the Prophetic Gifts of the Spirit in the Church Today*. Ann Arbor, MI: Servant Books, 1976.

Yohn, Rick. *Discover Your Spiritual Gifts and Use It*. Wheaton, IL: Tyndale House Publishers, Inc., 1974.

Zeller, George W. *God's Gift of Tongues*. Neptune, NJ: Loizeaux Brothers, 1978.

ENDNOTES

Chapter 2

1. Chafer, Lewis Sperry, *Systematic Theology, Pneumotology* (Dallas Seminary Press: Dallas, 1974., Page 246.

2. Vines, W. W., *Vine's Expository Dictionary of New Testament Words* (MacDonald Publishing Company: McLean), Page 159.

3. Strong, James, *Strong's Exhaustive Concordance of the Bible*, Page 24.

4. Ibid, Page 77.

5. Falwell, Jerry et al, *Liberty Commentary On the New Testament* (Liberty Press: Lynchburg, 1978., Page 77.

6. Innes, David, *I Hate Witnessing* (Visions House Publisher: Ventura, 1983., Page 197.

7. Drucker, Peter, *The Effective Executive* (Harper & Row Publishers: New York, 1966., Page 75.

Chapter 3

1. Stedman, Ray, *Body Life* (Regal Books, Glendale: 1972. Page 56.

2. MacArthur, John, *How to Know God's Will* (The Word of Grace Tape Ministry, Sun Valley, CA). Based on several points in MacArthur's outline.

Chapter 4

1. McRae, William, *The Dynamics of Spiritual Gifts* (The Zondervan Corporation: Grand Rapids, 1976. Pages 35-36.

2. Clinton, Bobby, *Spiritual Gifts* (West Indies Mission: Coral Gables, 1975. Page 7.

3. McSwain, Jay, *Finding Your PLACE In Ministry: Participant's Guide* (PLACE Ministries, Oklahoma City, OK, 2000) Page 15.

4. Ryrie, Charles, *The Holy Spirit* (Moody Press, Chicago: 1965. Page 83.

5. Ibid, Page 84.

6. This phenomenon was so great in the 1970s that the author wrote two manuscripts, one titled *The Other Gifts* and the other *How Important Should Spiritual Gifts Be in the Non-Charismatic Church?* Neither criticizes Pentecostal or Charismatic positions, but question the absence of practical teaching on the task-oriented gifts.

Chapter 6

1. Wagner, C. Peter, *Your Spiritual Gifts Can Help Your Church Grow* (Regal Books, Glendale: 1979., Page 177.

Chapter 7

1. Walvoord, John F., *The Holy Spirit* (Zondervan Publishing House: Grand Rapids, 1954/1958. Page 246.

2. Lightner, Robert P., *Speaking in Tongues and Divine Healing* (Regular Baptist Press: Schaumburg, 1965/1978. Page 10.

Chapter 8

1. Hauck, Gary L., *Is My Church What God Meant It to Be?* (Accent-B/P Publications: Denver, 1979. Page 77.

2. Wagner, C. Peter, *Your Spiritual Gift Can Help Your Church Grow* (Regal Books: Glendale, 1979. Page 40.

TEAM MINISTRY SPIRITUAL GIFTS RESOURCES
TO RELEASE THE POWER OF EVERYBODY

TEAM MINISTRY: How Spiritual Gifts Can Unleash the Power of Everybody—ISBN 978-1-57052-290-1 (for pastors and leaders) This 224-page book is a practical guide to help pastors and leaders unleash the power of their team through spiritual gifts. A perfect tool for ministry leaders who want to take their churches to new heights for God's Kingdom as it provides methods to help activate members' spiritual gifts, ways to use members' gifts to help your ministry grow, questions and tools for teaching the team gifts.

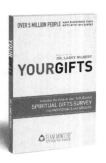

YOUR GIFTS: Discover God's Unique Design for You— ISBN 978-1-57052-289-5 (for individuals and small groups) This 192-page book is an indispensable companion to the *Your Gifts* Spiritual Gifts Survey (Survey contained in the book). It takes an in-depth look at each of the nine team gifts and will lead the user to go deeper in discovering God's unique design for them to become who God created them to be.

YOUR GIFTS: The Easy-to-Use, Self-Guided Spiritual Gifts Survey—ISBN 978-1-57052-286-4 (for adults) 16-page survey and gift summary plus answer sheet to help adults unwrap their God-given spiritual gifts so they can become the person they were meant to be! Discovering their unique giftedness and understanding spiritual gifts releases people to serve with effectiveness and fulfillment in the home, work, church and community.

YOUR GIFTS for Teens: The Easy-to-Use, Self-Guided Spiritual Gifts Survey—ISBN 978-1-57052-287-1
16-page survey and gift summary plus answer sheet to help teens discover their gifts and how to use them to fulfill God's plan for their life. What better time than now to understand how God desires to release them with passion and purpose as they begin to put these gifts into practice!

YOUR GIFTS for Children: The Fun, Easy-to-Use, Kid-Friendly Spiritual Gifts Adventure—
ISBN 978-1-57052-288-8

16-page illustrated guide of coloring pages and instruction to introduce children to spiritual gifts through Bible characters and the gifts they exhibited. This fun and insightful tool will help children learn how to grow closer to God through using their special gifts.

When individuals discover their unique giftedness, they can grow into the person God intends as they use their gifts in daily life and ministry . . . at home, church, school, work and beyond.
YOU ARE GIFTED by God to serve.

Available wherever Christian books are sold.
Your Gifts Spiritual Gifts Surveys are also available at special prices
for group or large-quantity purchases.

DR. LARRY GILBERT

has researched, written and
taught about spiritual gifts for
more than 40 years. As founder
of Ephesians Four Ministries
and Church Growth Institute,
Dr. Gilbert has worked with
tens of thousands of churches
and helped more than five
million people discover their
unique God-given gifts. Larry
and his wife, Mary Lou, have
three children and two grand-
children, and make their home
in Elkton, Maryland.